ONLY UNCLE

Olga Franklin

ONLY UNCLE

The story of Peter Lloyd Jeffcock
the bachelor with a
family of twelve

HUTCHINSON OF LONDON

HUTCHINSON & CO (PUBLISHERS) LTD
178–202 Great Portland Street, London W1

London, Melbourne, Sydney, Auckland
Bombay, Toronto, Johannesburg, New York

First published 1970

This book has been set in Baskerville, printed in Great Britain
on antique wove paper by R. J. Acford Ltd, Chichester, Sussex
and bound by William Brendon, Tiptree, Essex

ISBN 0 09 102510 9

CONTENTS

CONTENTS

ILLUSTRATIONS

With grateful acknowledgement for the help and information generously and freely given by former members and present members of the staff of the Children's Department of the LCC, now the Greater London Council.

FOREWORD

In 1958 the London County Council had 8,735 children in care, out of a total of 62,070 children in care in England and Wales. Children in care are those who for some reason have lost their homes or were born without one.

In 1965, just before the London County Council became the Greater London Council in April of that year, the LCC had 9,421 children in care; that is, 12.6 per 1,000 of their under 18 population. So altogether England and Wales had 67,099 children who had lost their homes and since then the figure had increased by about 1,000 children a year.

This is the true story of just 12 of the London children and what happened to them when they were handed over to the care of one man, to live with him in his romantic mansion in the country.

O.F.

INTRODUCTION

Peter Lloyd Jeffcock, the good-looking young bachelor who brought up 12 children, single-handed, was not what I expected.

Perhaps he was kidding, I suggested, and asked to see his housekeeper or lady help.

There was none, he said. Nor any wife? No, he'd never been married. Then where did he get the children?

He'd been given them, he said. By whom? By the LCC. He called it 'The Authority'. He meant the Greater London Council as it is now known.

This was my first conversation with him. I was sitting in Mr. Jeffcock's study-sitting-room in his attractive 17th-century farmhouse in Surrey, in the spring of 1969.

It all seemed a bit mysterious to me, in this ancient house with the dim-lit stone-flagged hall. I looked round the sitting-room which was pretty and cosy enough; the walls hung with some of his rather boyish paintings of small yachts in unknown harbours.

He was saying that the Council handed over the children to him ten years ago. They were nearly grown up now, some of them. At that time Local Government policy was to take children out of large institutions and convents, if they could find people to take them.

He's taken six girls and six boys and brought them up. He was their foster-father.

'You can come and meet some of them if you like; they're watching television in the next room. Yes, they're still living with me, most of them.'

I had to lean right back in the armchair to see his face. He was one of the most handsome men I had ever seen. As he stood up, he had to bow his head to avoid hitting it on the low-slung wooden beams across the ceiling. He was an immense figure, about six foot four inches in height, with thick dark hair and deep blue eyes. It was the kind of face and figure normally used to illustrate the coloured jackets of lady novelists' novels. His voice was true English public school.

'No, of course I'm not offended. But you do ask some rather Freudian questions,' he said. 'Aren't you ... forgive me ... rather narrow and prejudiced in your approach? That sort of thing depresses me.'

He sighed, rather heavily—a sort of groan. Then he led me next door to a smaller but much cosier room. A big fire burned; the room was uncomfortably hot. The TV set was on, very loudly. Around the room, on sofas and armchairs, sat six or seven young people. There were two girls with long flaxen hair hanging below their shoulders. They looked up smiling.

There was a small boy of about nine years of age and several tall youths, one with the fashionable long hair-do in a girlish bob. Peter Jeffcock introduced them.

'Pam, Christine, Paul, Brian, Denise, Babs, Simon ... Margaret.'

We returned to his room. So, it was true then. But why? Because he liked children?

'Of course, why else?'

Then why hadn't he married and had his own kids?

'There you go again,' he said, 'I didn't have time to get married as well, did I?'

He mentioned what hard work it'd been when they were young. Little girls with their bed-wetting; hours of washing-up for 13 and only Housewives' Choice to go with it. Sewing their dresses, washing school blouses and shirts, plaiting their hair, making curtains, cooking ...

How did it all begin?

Well, he'd once had a Grand Plan. To establish foster families of children, scores of them, all over south-east England.

The Plan failed. In all only three homes were started.

He was left with 12 children, to bring up as his own ... on his own.

The only really hard part, he said, had been people like me, coming to criticize, to doubt him.

They'd abused him, many of them. Even the 'Authority' sometimes thought him 'kinky'. At least, that was one of the politer words that were used about him.

Sometimes, in the past, people had stopped him in the street, in villages and country towns and said angrily: 'Why were these children, and all these girls given to you, a man? Why weren't they given to women to bring up?'

Sometimes he answered: 'Where are the women then?' Mostly, he ignored it. Let them talk; he didn't care what people said.

I spent months hearing Peter Jeffcock's story, right through, step by step.

This is my personal view of it in the following pages.

This is to say this is one woman's view of a good man who is also a better woman than most women are.

PART ONE

Peter Looks for the Children

The Boy

It was hard luck for Peter Lloyd Jeffcock that he was born good looking. Plain looks would have suited him much better, given the rather unusual ambition he had. This was not defined until much later. But it came to mean the longing to make life happier for as many children as possible.

Perhaps he was a bit of a saint really. And you don't need a handsome face and a six-foot-three-and-a-half-inch figure for it. In fact, it's a handicap. For one thing women have always noticed Peter and thought they could find better things for him to do.

It was rather like that situation told by Mr. Somerset Maugham in his novel The Razor's Edge, about the handsome young man who wanted to be a sort of saint. Pretty young women kept falling in love with him and trying to stop him.

Peter was born at Fern Lodge, Bracknell, Berkshire on the 30th December 1920 and his sister Pamela, two years later.

They were both strikingly handsome children, in their prams and afterwards. However, both soon became adept at dodging the too overwhelming embraces of admiring ladies in the neighbourhood.

Peter's father Philip Eric Jeffcock, an engineer who came from a well-connected Sheffield steel family, was educated at Malvern and Cambridge and distinguished himself, especially at sport. The late Philip Jeffcock was not only good looking but also remarkably strong. It was said of him that once, meeting a motorcar head on in some narrow country lane, and not liking the look of it, simply got out and without much effort or heavy breathing, turned the confronting car right round to face the opposite direction.

When his first wife died, nursing Belgian wounded in the First World War, he married Olive Lloyd, of Welsh origin, who had been orphaned as a child. She was reared in a way that was strict even for those times, that is the last decade of the century, in a boarding school under the care of a guardian who also had charge of a comfortable inheritance bequeathed by her Welsh grandfather, Harry Lloyd. She was orphaned at three years' old and two devoted spinster maids looked after her always.

She trained Peter and Pamela strictly too, in the way she herself was reared. She taught them, for instance, all the old-fashioned virtues of honesty and self-control and it left a lasting impression. Churchgoing was already declining in English villages in the '20s but the Jeffcock family never failed to appear at the Anglican church on Sundays.

It was not difficult for her to train her children as she thought fit, because for the first nine years she kept them by her side and did not send them to school. Mrs. Jeffcock taught them herself, with the result that both Peter and Pamela were in advance of their age in most subjects.

But it made for a lonely childhood. The family moved from one comfortable country house to another, settling at last at Little Park Hatch, Cranleigh, among the green fields and hills of Surrey.

In those days, it was a quiet place of great beauty. A very proper background for somewhat unwordly children like the Jeffcocks.

By the time he was nine, Peter was already very tall and immensely strong like his father. He was warned never to give his sister a push. Those hands and arms of his were stronger than any adult's. He grew up to be a charming, rather serious boy, very controlled for his age.

It was hard, though, for him with his energy and strength to sit sedately with his sister and parents round the fire in the evenings listening to the radio. He could already do crochet and embroidery just as efficiently as his mother. When his mother and Pamela took up knitting, he did the same! He got his own knitting-wool, needles and patterns and sat with them and knitted. Only he was faster and better at it. Whatever womenfolk could do, Peter could always do better . . .

He liked to be in the warm, bustling kitchen when his mother was cooking. He looked for small jobs to do to have the excuse for being there. He watched his mother stir puddings, make cakes, ice and decorate them for birthdays. It was not just that he was unconsciously learning how to do these things himself. Each movement and each task was as though photographed upon the boy's mind. He knew exactly how to hold a mixing-bowl, how to stir the creamed fat and sugar, how to bend down to the oven, even how to move between kitchen stove and table.

The boy lived each day intensely, savouring the ordered regularity of it, like the click-clack of the knitting needles. Oh, the green of those Surrey downs and hills and woods. Peter was a grateful boy.

He specially loved Christmas and the week which ended with his birthday, when the whole family went to stay with Grandma Firth at Welham near Retford. The rooks nesting in the big drive. The day of arrival at Grandma's house with its heavy, beautifully-turned brass handle. The scent of damp, stone walls and shrubs black in the clear Nottinghamshire air. And the nursery with its oil-stove sending flickering patterns across the ceiling. Sometimes there was a big fire burning in the bedroom grate. Peter knelt there, watching the flames. There was magic in that slowly oozing tar which made Nottinghamshire coal quite different from ordinary coal elsewhere.

At last the children were sent to school. Peter was almost ten years of age and already immensely tall. The first thing that happened was that the Headmaster stood Peter up against a door in front of the whole school, so that the boys could see the tallest pupil.

Peter always respected the rules, however bizarre. He even liked them. Rules, like having to walk on the left in the corridors, unless you belonged to a certain form with rights to stride up and down as you pleased. Up to a certain age, Cranleigh boys were obliged to wear their blazers buttoned up. On the other hand, your pyjama jacket must never be fastened at bedtime. A buttoned-up jacket was thought to be 'cissy'.

He was never a quarrelsome boy and no one was ever smashed to the ground by those great fists of his. But there was one memorable incident on prize-giving day at end of term. Peter forgot his usual caution upon shaking hands with the Headmaster, as he went to receive his prize. For a long time afterwards, the story went round that Peter had broken nearly every bone in the Head's hand. At any rate, that was the Head's story. Peter never enjoyed fighting, but he had to take part in the normal boxing lessons. He did this, however, without much enthusiasm.

The teacher said: 'I was waiting for Jeffcock to give that boy just one punch and the whole boxing contest would have been over.'

Peter got his house colours for running and proved to be a first-class rifle shot in the rifle shooting class. At rowing, he was superb and won many a heat in the boats.

In 1938, when Peter was 18, he decided that instead of going to Cambridge like his father, he would take up interior decorating. His mother was disappointed with his decision; she wanted him to be a doctor.

He took a job in the furnishing department at Harrods and a room in Kensington returning home to Cranleigh and his parents at the weekends.

This was the year when Peter claimed that for the first time and, perhaps, the only time, he fell in love. Her name was Susan; she was 16 and very pretty. They met at a party in Cranleigh; they also played tennis together.

He did not think of it as 'being in love' at the time. It was not really a thought that would have occurred to him. But later, after the war, when Susan was married to someone else, Peter met her again. Their meetings became a 'torture' to him. So then, Peter guessed that it must be love and he had missed it, probably forever.

2

The War

The war solved the problem of Peter's future for the present. He had already given up Harrods and interior decorating and the furniture department. Now he had a job on a farm in Kent and was set for a career in Agriculture.

In 1940 he volunteered. Peter was good at mathematics. The RAF sent him to Uxbridge to join a small, exclusive unit, to be known first as No. 8 AMES (Air Ministry Experimental Station). On June 1st 1941, the name was changed to No. 508 AMES. When the first instalment of this unit, which was rather a secret because it was engaged in experimental radar work, was shipped out to the Middle East Command (Haifa) on February 17th 1941, Peter Jeffcock went too and was heartily seasick throughout the voyage. The unit under the command of Flight Lieutenant Lachlan MacKinnon consisted of only 32 men, intelligent and good at mathematics. They moved to AHQ Egypt (Aboukir) in February 1942 and, in between, wandered the desert.

One of the men, a tall, slim youngster of 21 took a liking to Peter and liked teasing him about his great strength. This was Philip Birley, known as 'Pip'. Peter was called 'Jeff'.

'Jeff is the King Kong of our unit,' said Pip, 'with those great hands of his, like hunks of meat.'

Peter loved every minute of it. It was like being back at Cranleigh, except there were no corridors where you had to walk on the left. Peter and Pip used to stroll out into the desert at night, just to look at it, featureless, immeasurable. There was no right or left in the desert. There was the radio, however, and Lili Marlene. Above all, there were endless talks on Philosophy and Religion. Especially Religion. It was a very select unit.

Pip also noticed that Peter took with him always an ammunition case. In the huts where they slept, Peter kept the case beside him. One night Peter opened it and showed Pip the inside. There was no ammunition, no guns. It was filled with Peter's favourite books, novels and poetry. Peter read Charles Morgan's novel 'Sparkenbroke' over and over.

One night, there was a row between two of the men. Two service policemen, burly six-footers Bollard and Stockton. It became noisy and then it came to blows.

'Stop this immediately,' Peter called out to them. He was trying to read.

The men continued to fight.

Peter rose. 'For goodness sake, take your fight outside. You're becoming a nuisance.'

There was no response.

Pip Birley gasped as Peter moved to the two men, now scrapping on the floor. He picked them up, one in each hand, and carried them struggling outside the tent and threw them into the sand.

The whole unit never forgot that night. In future when things went wrong, if a generator broke down or someone got into trouble, the call went out 'Send for Jeff'.

Sometimes 'Jeff' drove alone into Benghazi to fetch whisky and beer for the unit. Often he noticed tiny children standing at street corners, a small hand cupped, outstretched. Peter always stopped his truck to give a child some sweets or to take a group of them for a ride away from the city stench.

When he was demobbed in November 1945, Peter went home to Cranleigh in a complex mood. It had been a nice war, he felt, for him. He sat in his old room where he'd slept as a boy and brooded. About suffering humanity mostly. He looked with some distaste at all his possessions, his books and old keepsakes, his quantity of leather articles, mostly birthday presents. His bedroom furniture was attractive too; but then he'd made a lot of it himself. It was just another knack he had, like knitting.

He still went to church on Sundays with the family. Those were the only times now when he wasn't brooding.

About the unfairness of life. About his problem. The problem was, he decided, how could he do some good in the world and show that he was grateful, truly grateful. For all that he had been given, including that 'nice war'.

For a year, on the suggestion of a family friend who, not unnaturally, admired Peter's looks, he took a year's drama course preparatory for RADA and a film career. Back to Cranleigh he went again still undecided, but feeling now he'd never make a film actor.

He wasn't ambitious he told his parents, and he wasn't interested in money.

'Peter keeps changing his mind,' Mrs. Jeffcock complained to her husband. But Peter's father was only mildly concerned. He saw that Peter resembled himself as a young man. He too, at that age, had always had a taste for helping people, for 'doing good'.

'Yes, Peter is like you', his mother said, 'quixotic like you. You were always a bit of a Don Quixote and Peter's just the same.'

At last Peter made up his mind. He joined the College of Estate Management, and went through a course of intensive study to qualify in Agriculture, Forestry and so on. This meant that he would be able to live quietly in the country and would earn a sufficient living as Estate Manager. He became friendly with a fellow-student who was a Roman Catholic. Without religion, he felt, no problem—whether of success or failure or loss—could be satisfactorily explained. In the end Peter decided to become a Catholic and he took instruction. One priest suggested that Peter might even become a monk. Peter declined, firmly, saying that he did not feel he was suited for life as a priest.

When he was qualified, Peter had no difficulty in obtaining work which meant living, of course, on the property. The work suited him and for a time, he was very happy. In the course of time, he became Manager of Property of a number of landed gentry, including Lord Hotham, the Earl of

Iddesleigh, Viscount Exmouth and others. He was living, as he always wanted, the life of a country gentleman.

It was in the early days, while working on one estate at Beverley, in Yorkshire that he had his first experience of how women were attracted to him, without his doing anything to encourage this. Perhaps Peter should have been warned by this experience, but it passed over him without his noticing anything wrong, until it was too late. After all there'd been lots of girls who'd come to take tea with his mother in the old days. There'd been Kathleen and Joan and Elizabeth and Nancy and, of course, Susan. There'd been a girl named Eva he'd met in Palestine, and a girl called Nadia. There was Margaret in Corsica. They were all nice girls. He enjoyed their company. He even corresponded with several of them.

His mother had been hopeful he might even marry one of them, especially from among those who came to tea at Cranleigh. But nothing ever came of it and they'd all gone off in the end and married someone else.

However, at Beverley he was very popular. He lived with the senior Estate Manager and his wife and children. And he became firm friends with them, especially with their children. This couple noticed how Peter was really very good with children.

They had to inform him, however, of the heartache and disappointment he had caused to two girls at Beverley. They were among others who always invited him to teas and dances and to go out riding.

He was astonished. Some people, he was told, felt he'd taken people's kind hospitality without giving anything in return.'

'You mean', said Peter, 'that they thought . . .?'

'Of course, they thought', said the Manager. 'You accepted all their invitations. You were always round there, for tennis or whatever. And the one girl . . .well you seemed to like her a lot. In fact we all thought . . .'

Peter said yes, yes, there was one girl who was very nice indeed. He liked her a lot. But it never entered his head. Marriage? After all, both this girl and the other one had both had plenty of other men friends as well. So why him?

It was all innocent and platonic, as always, but it left some bewilderment behind. Still he was moving on, now, to the next job. He was, he felt, always moving on.

The experience at Beverley ought to have been a lesson to Peter. Only it wasn't.

3

Disaster

It was 1950. Peter was 30. He got a job on a big estate in Northumberland.

At first he was immensely happy; happier than ever before. The countryside was beautiful to him. Peter had always felt strongly drawn to moors and hills.

Above all, the owner of the large estate, a Mr. Alexander, was a most simpatica personality. He and Peter became close friends. Mr. and Mrs. Alexander, with two small girls, were very kind to him. Perhaps the lady's kindness was so marked as, even then, to make him feel uneasy. But this, in all, was his happiest post so far.

During this time, a group of European refugee families moved into some old cottages on the estate, at Mr. Alexander's invitation. On his tours of the estate, Peter got to know them very well. Especially the children. A sort of mutual devotion sprang up. Peter began to call regularly, to see in what way he could help these poor families. He relished the idea of being helpful to these helpless creatures who seemed to have not the smallest idea of how to re-establish their lives.

He always had, with that enormous strength of his, far more energy than any ordinary job could contain. So there he was, day after day, doing little jobs to help them decorate the dilapidated dwellings. He was soon a favourite of the whole encampment. He took the children out for treats, driving them about in his land rover. He was like a Pied Piper among them. As soon as the tall figure appeared, striding across the open fields, the children ran towards him. It made him very happy. He began to think about ways he could improve life for them.

Then, quite suddenly, after a brief illness, the estate owner died. The wife's attitude became a great worry to Peter.

She was a dominating woman and a determined one.

Each morning she went in her dressing-gown into Peter's bedroom with his morning tea. Peter was at first embarrassed, then alarmed. 'But I don't like morning tea', he told her, 'I wish you wouldn't'. She seemed not to hear him. There was, at first, no lock on his door.

At night, she again entered his room with a tray containing a glass of hot milk. 'Thank you', said Peter as coldly as he dared, 'but I don't want any milk. I wish you wouldn't.'

Day after day this went on. It began to fray his nerves. He no longer even pretended to drink the tea, the milk. He felt that he was in a difficult even dangerous position. After all, she was the widow of his own great friend. She was only recently bereaved. He owed her respect, even kindness. But he felt towards her only fear.

Finally he could stand the tension and the worry no longer. He made a lock for his bedroom door. And the widow's attitude changed immediately. Some friends who came to stay sensed instantly what was happening.

'Have you seen how Peter looks? I think he is ill or anyway on the verge of a nervous breakdown. I don't think he gets anything to eat.'

It was true. Peter no longer appeared at family meals. Some of his friends among the refugees started taking food to Peter out in the fields where he worked sometimes.

And Peter wrote home: 'If it were not for their kindness to me I don't think I could have survived. I am now locked out of the house by nine o'clock at night.'

He could not eat. Some of the children made secret forays on the estate to find Peter and persuade him to drink the egg-nogs they took to him.

A more sophisticated man might have known how to deal with the situation. Peter thought if he kept out of the way, things might improve. He began to look pale and drawn and he got thinner every day. Clothes hung loosely on his huge frame. His mother wrote from Surrey, counselling him to give up the post as soon as his contract allowed.

Meanwhile things took a more serious turn. Slowly a campaign was building up against Peter, in which, clearly, the disappointed widow was the prime mover. It began first with whispers in the village. Then came shouts and rude words with the inference that he was a danger to the children. The refugee committee and the families themselves split up into two camps, those for Peter . . . and those against. Some took the widow's side. For she, too, took a close interest in them, their problems and their children. She was in fact chairman of the committee.

By this time Peter had moved out of the house and was living in a hotel in the village. The refugee children were now the only friends he had.

Peter continued taking some of the children out for rides and treats, just as he'd always done although about half the children were now forbidden to go near him. Walking through the village street was a torture to him. Even those who did not shout after him or call abuse at the tall figure going by, stared and stared . . . The country he loved so much had turned hostile towards him.

He was so isolated now. No girl friends like the pretty young things who had courted him at Beverley and Horley. Since moving into the great house on the estate, he had had no need of any other friends apart from the owner, now dead, his wife and their children.

Finally his health broke. He resigned his job. It was discovered that the widow was planning a ceremonial send-off with a lunch party for him. Perhaps she wanted to show her magnanimity. One of the Estonian families broke the secret to Peter.

Instead, two taxi-load of cottagers and children foiled her by taking him off to the station themselves and giving him a rousing send-off.

One wrote to Peter: 'When she found out you'd gone with our send-off instead of hers, all hell broke loose.'

Peter went home to his parents in Surrey. For six weeks

he stayed in bed or loafed at home; he was a broken man, his hopes shattered.

Yet already an idea was forming in his mind. Despite his present misery, or perhaps even BECAUSE of it, he was beginning to formulate a plan.

He had first described it in letters home and now he put it in letters to his Catholic friend who was now a priest.

'I began to see that this was what I wanted to do; to give a good home to poor children like these.

'I was appalled to see the conditions in which they often lived, with fungus growing on the walls of their huts or caravans.

'Yet I also saw that no matter how shocking and decayed the home, the children could thrive where they had love from their parents and where they could feel secure.'

Some weeks later an offer came of an excellent opening: to run the Estates of three separate concerns, the University of Wales at Aberystwyth, and those of Lord Iddesleigh and Lord Exmouth.

Peter pulled himself together. Outwardly calm and contained, he moved into the Bellevue Royal Hotel at Aberystwyth. First he checked there was a lock on the bedroom door. Never again would he sleep peacefully in a room which had no lock upon his door.

He was under contract for the next four years and worked freelance also. He was able to save some money, though he got into the habit of spending on fast cars, including two classic Rolls-Royce cars. He was a good driver and a fast one.

But he was turning more often for comfort to the Catholic church.

One day Peter was recalled by the RAF for a refresher course to last a fortnight. He was sent to an island off the coast of East Anglia. In his pockets he carried some advertisements he had cut from Catholic newspapers and magazines.

When he was alone, Peter took them out and read them again. It seemed extraordinary that there were so many of them. Quite a little pile now. He knew that there were deprived children but he never expected there could be so many.

One advertisement read: 'Foster home wanted for two children aged seven and eight, boy and girl whose parents have recently divorced. Please apply to Area Children's Officer, County Hall.'

He made up his mind that when he got back from the island, he would do something about the advertisements. He would first find out more about these children. Who were they, where did they come from and how could he help? He decided he would write or telephone.

He sat with a pencil and pad and started to compose a reply to several of the advertisements, including one for a family of seven children from Birmingham.

Some men might have been marked by an experience so shattering as that with the widow of his best friend. Shunned by a whole village, outlawed by his employers . . .

Some men might have lived in such a way that never again could anyone point at him, single him out, abuse him . . .

On Peter it had quite the opposite effect. He would show them, all of them. If it meant martyrdom again, then so be it . . .

4

Search for the Children

In the next five years, County Hall which was then the headquarters of the London County Council and many other Children's Departments of local authorities in south-east England, came to know the name of Peter Lloyd Jeffcock.

Constantly he was writing and telephoning with suggestions for looking after the children. Just as constantly, he was disappointed. This was no surprise. Unworldly as he still was, even Peter knew that an unmarried man in his early 30s was not the person most likely to recommend himself to a local authority. It was even more unlikely when Peter had to admit that he had no special qualification or training for the job of caring for children. Nor was it any recommendation that he had decided to abandon his chosen profession of estate management to do it!

Oh, he was bursting with ideas! But alas, it was cosy solid homes equipped with loving Mums and Dads that were needed; not ideas.

Nevertheless, Peter kept on. He was now living in a small flat in London. On hearing of his new plans to provide homes for children, his mother, deciding that perhaps after all her only beloved and attractive son might well be a bit unbalanced, made no comment. Peter's father also said nothing. Well brought-up English people always did behave in this way; that is to say, they hid their disappointments and said . . . nothing.

At this time, Peter worked as a free-lance estate manager, doing occasional jobs when they appealed to him; driving one of his classic Rolls fast across the country—always keeping an eye open for suitable houses in the country which he might buy in order to develop his schemes for the children.

He had other interests too. He made during this period, nine trips to Lourdes, acting as courier for parties going on pilgrimage. He was doing this for St. Christopher Tours of Thurloe Place, London, and he became very skilled at caring for the coach parties which made the five-day trips to Lourdes for about £35 each. As usual, people always re-marked how grateful they were for the special kindness and interest he showed in the children.

When not on duty, Peter visited the Grotto and prayed. He specially loved the Easter tours. He saw nothing odd in his own tall, healthy figure bowed alongside the sick and the crippled, there in the Grotto. If he prayed for a miracle, it was not for himself, but for those so far unknown lost and missing children whom he would one day rescue. The tall figure was sometimes seen at Lourdes, taking a party of nuns out to dinner. He always got on well with the Good Sisters.

He also joined a Catholic Dining Society; having decided it was time for him to reappear, so to speak, in society. There were charming little dinner parties in the Rembrandt Hotel. There was even a new girl friend. A pretty girl named Rosamond. But she was rich. Her family stopped it by rushing her off to marry a man of their choice.

So, once again, Peter was snatched, so to speak, from the very jaws of marriage (he was fond of Rosamond and marriage was mentioned).

And the search for children was on again.

And always his pockets were stuffed with the details of advertised children.

The years went by . . . and the dream children in their dream homes, seemed further away than ever.

The plan, with which Peter tried year after year to tempt the local authorities, was this:

He would buy property; country houses. For this he had a special knowledge, due to his profession as manager of property for landowners which he had successfully pursued for some years in Northumberland, Cardiganshire, Devon-shire, Yorkshire and other parts of Britain.

There would be 'good women' coming from all over Britain, to be put in charge of these houses and to look after the children.

He would plan, organize and finance it. On top of that, there would be the maintenance money from the Authority. He had, already, tentatively discussed with an insurance company, the prospect of borrowing up to £30,000 in the next year or so, with which to buy houses suitable for these 'good women'. The idea was that, then, under his supervision, as boss of his Housing Scheme, the women would settle down to family life, in their own house, each with a family of foster-children.

He hoped, eventually, to establish as many as a hundred such families. In each home, there would be not more than six or eight children, in order to secure family life . . . in contrast to the Institutional life to which such children were condemned.

'All would be done', Peter said, 'within the framework of Local Authority rules, regulations, financial support and responsibility. If it comes off, just think, we can find homes for 800 kids. That is, 800 out of the 80,000 without homes at present.'

As for finance, Peter had got that all worked out. He would obtain the houses through an extensive mortgage, combined with his own capital, large enough in the long run to form a separate housing association or similar body. Thus, he would be enabled to buy more and more houses and to look for more and more good women. Each good woman would get a house for her 'life-time'.

The necessary maintenance money would be collected from each Local Authority and handled by a single body, and given to each family as housekeeping every week.

He, Peter Jeffcock, would also establish certain rules of his own. In each family, there must be both boys and girls, older ones and younger ones; the oldest having the right never to be superseded by the introduction of others older than themselves.

And then . . . it happened. In the autumn of 1958, nearly seven years after the misery of his experience with the refugee children, the plan at last began to take shape.

For, driving about the country as usual in his classic Rolls Royce car, he saw a possible house! It was a 15th-century manor house called Kinnersley Manor, standing in seven acres. The cost of the property was £10,000.

It was a romantic sort of place. He was a romantic man. So he bought it.

This was the place where one day he would, please God, bring the children home.

5

First of the Good Women

Dreams of Good Women and 100 Houses did not, however, really make the right appeal to Children's Departments.

While negotiations for Kinnersley Manor were pending, Peter was once again assigned by St. Christopher's Tours to join five other couriers for conducting 180 people, paying £400 each, for the round trip from the West Indies to Le Havre, through France, Belgium, Switzerland, Italy and Britain.

During the Lourdes part of the tour, Peter became friendly with one of the tourists, Anne Stewart-Spence. Anne was a dark attractive woman approaching 40 who worked as secretary to a microbiological institute in Trinidad. Her father, a Scot, had formerly managed a sugar estate in Dutch Guiana. For her the trip was something slightly more than a holiday tour of Europe. Trinidad was about to be federated. British and other foreign support of the institute might be withdrawn. She knew that if she did go home, where she had no relatives, she might find her job was ended. Meanwhile she hoped to visit relatives in Scotland.

Anne was travelling with friends made on the tour, a women named Olga Nicol and her adopted daughter Pamela. One evening they were discussing Peter.

'What a unique man he is,' Anne was saying. 'Have you noticed how marvellous he is with the children in all the coaches?'

The others said that everyone had noticed this. They said they also noticed that Anne was very much attracted to Peter.

'Of course, I'm attracted,' said Anne who always spoke plainly what she was thinking. 'From the very first moment I set eyes on him, I thought "Ah, there's a handsome man. . . ." '

However, Anne Spence was not the kind of woman to push herself or to try and distract Peter from his ardent ambition. Whenever they met, it was to discuss the possibilities of Peter's plan. And Miss Nicol or Nikky, as she was called, and Pamela were also interested in it.

Peter told them that things were moving at last. He told them about the house, Kinnersley Manor, which he had found for his starting-off point. He told them the cost of the property and that he was able to manage this partly with his own money and partly with a loan from the Westminster Bank. By coincidence, the house was near Horley where his parents and sister now lived, after moving from Cranleigh.

At the end of the tour, they parted with arrangements to meet in London.

It was a beginning anyway. He longed to get started on re-organizing Kinnersley Manor. He saw, in imagination, Anne installed as Mother of one house; perhaps Nikky and Pamela for another house he would soon be buying. At last, at last!

He saw the plan extending in his imagination. With himself, overall, as Administrator. He thought of how he would go contentedly from house to house, carrying gifts and the housekeeping money. He thought of women with warm, attractive faces like Anne's, standing at the porch of weathered farmhouses, saying 'Yes, all the children are getting on very nicely, thank you.'

Back home again he felt a renewal of his old energy, as he plunged into the work of turning Kinnersley Manor into a combined Guest House and family house. It was Christmas 1958 and Peter was not the kind of man to telephone builders and plumbers . . . and then sit back and wait for the result.

Kinnersley Manor had three floors. Peter's idea was to turn as much as possible of the building into self-contained flats. The money from the paying-guests would help to finance the family part of the house into which he would put his children . . . when he got them.

With the same facility with which he knitted and embroidered and sewed as a boy, he turned to the multiple jobs of electrician, plumber, carpenter, builder. In one flat, he installed a kitchen sink, connected it to the drains, connected a water supply, fitted a Calor gas stove (as there was no mains gas). He installed altogether four gas stoves of standard size at £40 each. As soon as one flat was ready, he telephoned the agents. The house was soon filled with tenants.

Soon Anne arrived to cook and look after the tenants generally. She wrote to friends in Trinidad that she had decided to stay in Britain and work for 'this wonderful person who wants to do this thing for humanity'. She was referring to the children to whom she would become Foster Mother when she got them from Peter who would get them from the Council.

This, then, was the plan and how it began. It never seemed to occur to Peter at this time, nor to Anne or to anyone else concerned, that perhaps all the good, kind, motherly women might never turn up. Or if they did turn up, they might not stay.

For at that time, the house day after day seemed packed to bursting with good and helpful women. Nearly all were friends whom Peter had met on the tours to Lourdes. So often they'd heard him talk, hopefully, about his plans. Now they arrived on the doorstep at Kinnersley all eager to help.

There was Edith who could not make up her mind what 'to do with her life'. She'd tried being a postulant in a convent but later returned to the world. In many ways, she was like Peter himself; that is she could do more with one hand than most people with two. Edith swept through the house like a whirlwind, scouring, scrubbing, dusting and polishing. She carried furniture up and down three floors. It was nothing to Edith to transport a wardrobe, single-handed, down four flights of stairs like a practised removal man. When night came and others flopped, Edith was still at it . . . with bucket and pail.

There was Margaret who arrived from Yorkshire with her aunt. Margaret had met Peter in Lourdes three years earlier and she was eager to help. Also from Lourdes there was Carmel with her parents who all came to help make the house clean and tidy.

The women friends and helpers arrived with much eagerness and active enthusiasm. As they waited for the children to arrive, they planned and organized, scrubbed and polished. The days turned into weeks. No children came. In the end they drifted away, until only Anne remained.

It was typical too that when the Post Office forgot to install a telephone for the cottage, which stood on the estate, Peter simply did it himself. The tenants there were a pilot, Mr. Kirwan, his doctor wife and two children. Peter had tried telephoning the Post Office without result. In the end he found a telephone from somewhere and connected it up to the one in the big house!

So the New Year passed in a flurry of preparation. January, February, March and April came and went. So many friends had left, the house seemed empty.

And still no children. . . .

6

Peter Hears about his First Child

Father Woolmer called from the local Catholic church. Peter was gloomy. 'Everything is ready, but where are the children? Sometimes I think it will never happen.'

Father Woolmer said that Peter must not lose heart. Fortunately he still had plenty to do. There was no gardener, so Peter mowed the lawns and banks. He bought six Jersey heifers to roam the seven acres beyond the house and these he fed and kept clean himself. But for milk supplies every day he went to the local farm up the lane and returned with a cream churn, fresh from the dairy, filled with Guernsey milk topped with cream.

It made Peter sad when he distributed the milk to his tenants that he still had no children of his own to drink the lovely stuff.

He tried to keep busy and not to think about his perpetual worry that perhaps the children would never arrive. He made curtains on his own sewing-machine for Anne's room, painted the walls, stained the floor and made some of the furniture too.

Between these jobs, he sat down to write more letters to the 'Authority', as he always called the LCC. By June, he was getting desperate and started writing to Children's Departments outside London. There were seven children in Birmingham. Peter wrote, hopefully, asking for them. The reply came, as usual, 'Thank you. No.'

He wrote again: 'I have for a long time been discussing foster children with various departments in England, because I have been working on a scheme for the care of Catholic children in need of a home, for some years now. I have reached the point where a home can be offered to a number of these children. . . .

'The position here is that this very large house is divided

into the main portion which serves as a private house, and several cottages and flats. In the main house I hope to establish a family of children, about eight or ten in number. These will be cared for by those who run the house, as in a private family where one employs nurse-maids to look after the children. In this case, however, I am not married, and propose simply to act as a Foster Father and generally as an administrator, since we hope to expand elsewhere in due course.'

Peter wrote this letter in reply to an advertisement in the local press, which sought a foster home for four children of one family at present being cared for in a convent.

So the summer passed, peacefully, except for the frustration of moving about his comfortable house and now beautiful garden, yet still empty, empty. . . .

He was not to know that it was the last summer he would spend as a childless man. He was waiting for something to happen.

At last something did.

It was Father Woolmer who brought the first news. The LCC were looking for a home for a 13 year old boy at present in the care of a local school. He related how a Child Care Officer had called on him at the Presbytery.

By this time Peter knew only too well what was the role of a Child Care Officer. He knew them all . . . from top rank of Children's Officer which is the Head of the Department, through Senior Child Care Officer who were responsible for the CCOs (as they were always called) down to the CCOs themselves.

Anyway the name of the CCO was Albert Roads and he wanted to know if Father Woolmer knew of anyone willing to offer the boy a permanent home.

The next step was that Mr. Roads called at Kinnersley Manor. Peter invited him into his study, and offered him a drink.

The two men sat down to talk about the future of John,

who had no parents and no home and was slightly backward. Mr. Roads said that the Children's Department felt that John would not improve his education until he had a stable background and homelife. He had been moved from one foster home to another, one school to another. What was needed was a good home for good.

'And that,' said Mr. Roads, 'means, as you know, someone who will take care of John until he is 18 at least. All his life he has been in the care of the LCC.'

'I understand,' said Peter. After years of study of all the LCC regulations concerning the welfare of deprived children, Peter could have said them all off by heart anyway.

'Well?' said Mr. Roads. 'According to Father Woolmer, you are intending to use your house for the benefit of such children.'

'That is so,' said Peter, 'only so far we haven't got any children.' And he laughed. A rather bitter laugh though.

Mr. Roads's reply to that was to ask if he could take a look round the house and garden. He then left, saying he would report back to the Department to say that, as far as he could tell, there was no reason why the boy should not come to live with Peter at Kinnersley Manor.

Was it possible, after all the waiting, the planning and hoping of the past six years, that after all it was going to come true?

Could you really get a child . . . just like that, after a nice chat and a drink with a CCO?

Nothing happened for another six weeks. Then a letter arrived from the LCC. The Children's Officer, Mr. Denis Allen, would very much like to call and bring with him the Department Inspector, Mr. Michael A. Fitzgerald.

The two LCC officers came to tea on July 15th and spent the afternoon chatting with Peter in his study.

It was the first time Peter had such a chance to describe his plan in detail . . . to such an audience. He was determined to leave nothing out!

The 13 year old boy John was almost forgotten as Peter launched into it. He hoped to find people to look after families of eight children, of all ages, boys and girls. The ages should be spread about as much as possible to 'match' a typical natural family. Each family must contain not less than three children who were 'permanent' in the sense that there was no one, no parent or relative, who would take them back at any time.

He wanted the foster-parents protected against the heart-breaking loss of the children; or at any rate the *total* loss of all the children. He wanted to create families where children would develop family ways and customs as in a natural family. He talked of the rights of children, of parents; he talked of affection and public opinion.

Peter talked on and it was clear he believed deeply in every single word of it.

7

The Men from the LCC

The men from the London County Council motored back to London from Kinnersley Manor, puzzled and slightly overwhelmed.

They still had to decide what to do about the boy John. Could they trust this extraordinary man? What kind of man was he anyway? Would his enthusiasm last, or was he kidding himself?

Peter always said that if it had not been for Denis Allen, the whole story might never have happened.

Certainly it was Allen who made the first moves. He was a man almost as unique as Jeffcock, and like Peter he was also exceptionally attractive.

He was a Quaker who, while working as a Cable & Wireless clerk during the war, started to do voluntary work to help refugee children from the Continent.

He had always cared deeply about children since he and his four kid brothers lost their own home and were sent to a boarding school. After the war, he joined the LCC and worked as an Area Children's Officer, covering about one-ninth of the LCC area. This meant that he was responsible for about 900 children, chiefly in the Wandsworth and Battersea areas.

His boss at that time was a Mr. Michael A. Fitzgerald, always known as 'Fitz', a man also devoted to children who had worked for years in residential schools and had immense experience. Fitz had the rank of Department Inspector, and he was also unmarried. Ultimately, the decision belonged to Fitz and in the following weeks, they talked of little else, while trying to make up their minds what to do.

They knew that no ordinary foster home would do for John who had already been ill-treated in one such home.

The boy was slightly backward too, from having been moved so often from one foster home to another.

Their dilemma was that they had to take risks all the time. Yet they knew that some children were suffering anyway, so the gamble seemed smaller. It wasn't a case of taking children who were already in very good care and who were all right and suddenly exposed them to danger.

Convent life varied a lot. Some children were suited to it but for others they were pretty barren places. Denis visited them all the time. He told Fitz about one visit to a school for sub-normal children of all ages up to 16. 'I was greeted very well and given a meal. But as I sat there, there were 100 children passing that door behind me without my knowing they passed because they went in utter silence. What life is it, Fitz?'

Denis knew that he could always put children into a Monastery and they would be brought up safely by the Brothers. And he and Fitz would be safe too! No one could ever say they took risks with children because monasteries and convents were respectable places and recognized by the church. But the children who grew up there might, in the end, become inadequate people, unable to give and receive love. The places themselves were all right, but they were just too big!

So the two men argued and discussed in the weeks that followed. And in the end Fitz decided. They would do it, they would give Peter his chance. It was a gamble, yes, but it was worth it.

Why? Denis has since answered that question.

'If it had been left to me alone, I might well not have done it', said Denis. 'Possibly not. Having somebody else say, "Yes, I think it's safe", decided the whole thing.'

'Fitz was an Inspector of Child Care and a man whose judgment I trusted implicitly. Fitz himself was a single man, about my age, and did superb work with adolescent boys. I think he was probably disposed not to say automatically that single men were too dangerous to use. I had a great regard for Fitz. For both his character and his work. So I was in the same mental condition.

'We thought Jeffcock eccentric but we both thought it was clear that he was a man with a vocation who could just as well have been a priest as run a children's home. And had he become a priest, no one would have made insinuations against him.

'And in the end I came to see what Peter Jeffcock really was. I saw him as one of the Knights of Chivalry, something belonging to centuries past.

'The thing about Peter was he was prepared to offer something we couldn't get elsewhere. At the time, I had great doubts about whether it would last. I thought he might be kidding himself; I mean about his endurance.

'But the thing which worried me most in a way was his rather grandiose ideas for running homes . . . a hundred of them! He kept trying to recruit these women.'

Denis explained that the Authority were always wary of too dedicated women, devoted to children. Sometimes it meant the women were violently possessive. And that wouldn't do, because many of the kids did have one parent or even both parents and relatives somewhere and possibly might go home one day.

'When Peter recruited a woman, he'd telephone to tell us about her and we'd go down and have a look at her. On the whole, those who were the most casual were the ones we liked best, and Peter liked least! We were afraid that the devoted ones he did like, wouldn't let the children have their own lives and this could possibly be dangerous.

'Nevertheless, we appreciated what HE was offering. He was offering a positive thing. He was ready to provide a home which really cared for children 24 hours a day, with no changes of staff. No one coming off duty and someone else going on. And yet it would be without the too close emotional involvement which often causes breakdowns in foster homes.

'There weren't many people like Peter. Peter had a great

capacity for affection, which children would respond to, and he had a good brain. He knew their needs on different levels; he could intellectualize them and meet them. It wasn't simply a question of mother love.

'Of course, we were worried; of course we had doubts. We had a hunch; we took a chance. Not only about was he a sound man, but was it going to be permanent.

'Oh yes, we've been asked: why did you risk it? Well, we had 900 children in our care and we knew some were being deprived, even though they got three meals a day; they were deprived of love. Not through deliberate intention; it just was not possible.

'If I'm asked, finally, would I take a risk or be safe and certainly deprive children of love, then, yes, I'd have to take that risk. And then, Father Woolmer came along and said, "Have you been to see Mr. Jeffcock? He's sitting out there at Kinnersley Manor waiting for something to happen".'

And so they decided. And it did all start to happen.

8

The First Five

Peter was expecting his first child, John, to arrive and was busy preparing a room in the attic, making a bookcase and filling it with books, when the telephone rang. Miss Smith wanted to speak to Mr. Jeffcock.

She had four children to offer, all of one family now living at St. Vincent de Paul Convent, Mill Hill, in North London. Margaret the eldest, age eleven had been there seven years with her sister Babs, age nine. Their two brothers Terry (eight) and Willy (seven) had arrived there two years earlier from a convent in Brighton.

Miss Smith explained that the Authority (the LCC of course) wanted to move the children to a permanent home but it wasn't easy to find a home for all four together. Would Peter like to meet them? Peter would. He was invited to visit the convent to see them.

Clearly, word had gone—like wildfire so to speak—that Mr. Jeffcock was okay. After all, if Denis and Fitz said so . . .

Peter took his sister Pamela in his Land Rover. The children were neatly dressed. The Mother Superior presented them, and a party of nuns waved through the window as Peter drove the whole party into the shopping-centre to look for a tea-shop.

Seated round the table loaded with a huge pot of tea, bread, jam and cakes, Peter looked at his first children. The little boys were good looking with shining, black hair which waved. Babs was a tiny strawberry-blonde freckled all over and spoke with a lisp so pronounced that her excited comments had to be translated by Margaret to be understood.

Peter's heart sank when he looked at Margaret. So soon his noble ideals were to be put to the test. Peter liked pretty

children, but at that age Margaret was far from pretty. She
had a lisp too, but, clearly, she was the one who did the
talking.

Characteristically therefore, Peter set himself out to try
hard to like Margaret.

'Would you like some more sugar in your tea, Margaret?'
Peter said. Like the others she had already put six lumps
into one cup.

'You said we could', said Margaret, 'you said we could
have as much sugar as we liked.'

'Babs took the last', said Terry.

'Leave Babs alone', said Margaret, immediately on the
defensive. Margaret had been trained ever since she could
speak to look after the interests of her sister, Babs, two years
younger.

'Of course, you can have as much as you like', said Peter.
The sugar bowl was refilled with more lumps, several lumps
going into each child's cup while at the same time they
popped the remainder straight into their mouths. The bowl
was soon empty again.

Peter and Pamela were quite charmed with the skill shown
in this operation. For even while the sugar lumps diminished,
the children kept the conversation flowing, despite having to
suck hard at the same time. Terry, the elder of the two boys,
turned wide, innocent grey eyes on the grown-ups, and smiled
without revealing two lumps held in either cheek.

'Are you going to take us back to the convent?' he said.

'Can we go for a ride first?' said Babs through her lisp.

'Oh yes, can we?' said Willy, with a flick of the wrist,
disposing of the last two sugar lumps into his mouth.

'It's a very nice convent,' Peter said.

'Oh yes,' said Babs.

'Very nice,' said Willy.

'Sister's lovely,' Babs lisped.

Terry put a hand on Peter's arm.

'Take us with you,' Terry said.

'Then we'll go back after,' said Margaret.

Willy clung to his other arm.

'We've not been in a car', he said, 'not ever.'

'All right.' Peter stood up.

The children clapped and cheered.

People were staring.

In fact, they were quite ordinary children and behaved very well on this exciting occasion. But Peter, letting his eyes slide away unseeing from Margaret's squint behind her National Health spectacles, thought the whole afternoon delightful. Especially, the sugar bowl and the way it disappeared. Peter knew that in the convent there was a strict limit on how much you were allowed to take on to your own plate and into your own cup.

When the telephone rang again six weeks later, it was Miss Smith of the LCC to say that the children were his.

It was as easy as that! All the dossiers on each child had been made out by the convent and sent to the Authority. The children had been through their 'medical'. The papers were complete with all the details filled in; why their home had broken up, their behaviour record and whether they'd ever had any fits.

At midday on Friday, Peter drove back to the Convent. The same nuns in the huge butterfly head-dress showed him into the sitting-room of the Mother Superior. The convent which was a day and boarding-school was vast and shining and impersonal.

Peter thought he noticed the Mother Superior watching him with a critical glance. Tea was brought.

'Well, Mr. Jeffcock,' she said, 'I hear that you want to have our children. What sort of house have you got? I see, and who lives there? Are you married? No, I see.'

Peter was embarrassed. He could see very well that the Mother Superior simply did not see and that the whole set-up was very difficult to follow.

'But the house is full of people just now,' he said quickly, to cover up the awkward moment. 'And there is a very

D

nice woman Anne Spence staying there just now whom I
met at Lourdes. No, she doesn't do anything specific; just
staying.'

Peter rattled on, saying anything that occurred to him.

'We have some—er—heifers', Peter said, 'and a hen.'

There was a silence, Mother Superior waited.

'And some tortoises in the garden.' He stopped suddenly.
He felt sorry for her. After all, Mother Superior had been
responsible for the children all these years. They'd been
here and now she had to hand them over to a strange young
man.

However, it was not her responsibility. That belonged to
the Authority. The children belonged to the State, the all-
powerful State, he thought grimly, remembering he had
waited nearly as long for these children as Jacob waited for
his bride Rachel.

The four children were brought in, neat and clean in
their new grey school uniforms from the LCC clothing issue.
Peter noticed that Margaret's clothing did not fit at any
point.

Peter could see that the Mother Superior wanted to put
more questions. Some of the nuns came bustling in to kiss
the children goodbye. They crowded at the window to wave
as Peter settled them into the Land Rover.

Mother Superior stood on the porch. 'We hope you will
all be very happy with Mr. Jeffcock,' she said.

'And I hope that too', said Peter as he started the car.

'Sister said you're a very nice man and you're taking us
to a very nice place,' said Margaret; she was still nervous
of this strange man and thought she ought to make the effort
to please, for the sake of the others.

Peter was silent, trying to control an unreasoning rush of
impatience. He must, he felt, learn to be patient with this
unattractive child. She was entitled to the affection which
he had promised to all of them. Probably it was that awful
coat she was wearing; it made her look dumpier than
ever.

The children looked somehow very small in the great hall of Kinnersley Manor. They rushed about excitedly, each clutching their cardboard suitcases containing all their possessions and souvenirs, including the three new sets of underwear and other garments provided by the LCC clothing depot.

Babs was the boldest. She managed to push open heavy doors and peeped in.

'Sssss—look Mag,' said Babs, 'It's just like the Sisters', all big and shiny.'

'Uncle didn't say you could,' said Margaret piously, 'Did you, uncle? Did you say we could go all over?'

'What was Babs saying Margaret?' Peter hoped he would soon learn to cure Babs' lisp.

He was touched to see that Terry kept his arm protectively round Willy's shoulder.

After tea, Peter took them up to their rooms. He had put twin beds in rooms with his own room in the middle. The beds, he thought, looked quite pretty with the children's eiderdowns he had bought specially. He busied himself around the rooms, supervising their unpacking.

'Is this one mine?' said Willy, opening his chest of drawers. 'And this one's mine?' said Terry, rushing across the room.

Peter was enjoying himself. He knew that at the convent they had never owned anything. Even an empty cupboard was exciting.

Margaret was fussing about, unpacking Babs' teddy-bear and asking to see where Babs' things were to be put. Margaret's unrelenting care for Babs was getting tedious.

At eight p.m. he said goodnight to each child. He was careful not to kiss them. He would wait, he promised himself, until they wanted to kiss him.

When the door closed Margaret said in a whisper 'Babs —are you all right?'

'Yes.' Bab's lisp was so strong it came out like a hiss.

'Babs!'

'What is it?'

'What's that funny noise?'
'Shut up—he said no talking!'
'Babs—do you like him?'
'He's all right.'
'Willy's scared—he wet himself.'
But Babs was snoring slightly.

Next morning Peter was woken about six o'clock by a dreadful noise. At least, it sounded dreadful for he had never heard anything like it before. He lay in bed and listened, horrified.

It was only the noise of children talking and banging about excitedly. But in his peaceful country house it sounded to him quite thunderous.

Anyway, no more sleep. He got up and went to the children's rooms.

'What is going on, Margaret?'

He realised how unfair it was to pick on Margaret, glowering in her utility issue pyjamas and squinting sourly without her NHS spectacles.

'We were only looking through the windows. Look Babs, cows over there.'

It was clear that they had never seen any Jersey heifers in the London convent school. Peter softened slightly.

Terry and Willy were still leaping about, opening and shutting doors and cupboards.

'There's no roads nor streets,' said Babs, looking out at the green fields.

Peter was glad that they were not frightened, or it seemed even very impressed with him so far.

'Now', said Peter, clearing his throat carefully, 'now that I am going to be your Uncle and you are going to live with me for always, I have to make certain rules. For example when you wake up in the morning, you are not to talk or to make a noise. So no talking till I am up and come to fetch you. Remember we have Paying Guests in the house. Besides I have to have some rest too, you know.'

'If Babs wants to go somewhere, what shall I do?' said
Margaret who appeared to have no other interest in life
than in protecting Babs' interests.

'Babs can go quietly on her own,' said Peter. 'And now
all get dressed and come quietly down to breakfast.'

'What shall we wear?' said Babs. The children crowded
round him. They had never had any choice before. But now,
there were the extra new garments from the LCC clothing
store.

Peter helped the girls get into their grey pleated skirts
and the boys into their grey shirts and pullovers.

At breakfast he felt for the first time deeply excited. Now
he had a family. He might even get to like the dreadful
noise in time. If only the children didn't all speak at once.
What they would do after breakfast, what they could see
outside, how far could they go from the house, etc. etc. It
was the first time in their lives they'd had a choice.

Peter felt suddenly very nervous, as three of the children
rushed away into the garden, leaving him sitting with the
dour face of Margaret. Why didn't she go with them? It
really was too bad of her. How would he ever learn to love
this difficult child?

He resolved he would try though. It was his duty. After
all, he loved all children everywhere, didn't he? They
couldn't all be beautiful and attractive. If he didn't learn
to love and understand Margaret then the whole thing, the
whole marvellous plan had been a ghastly mistake.

In future, he decided, he would refuse to see a child in
advance. He was determined to accept every child sent by
the Authority, no matter what, to try with all his might to
love those he didn't like. After all, he told himself, there was
no such thing as an unlikeable child, though some were
handsome and some weren't.

The next day was Saturday and John arrived. He came
up the drive with his CCO, Mr. Albert Roads.

Peter met them in the hall and shook hands. Mr. Roads

said: 'Goodbye for now John. I hope you'll be happy with Mr. Jeffcock.'

Afterwards Peter introduced John to his new four brothers and sisters. It all passed off quite well, Peter thought. Fortunately, John was a very quiet boy and didn't really seem to have anything to say at all.

9

Learning Country Style

In the next fortnight Peter took the children out and bought them all new clothes. He enjoyed this just as much as they did.

He spent all his own money, of course, because nothing had arrived yet from the Authority.

He bought striped pyjamas for the boys and the girls got their first nightdresses they'd ever owned.

The children were excited over their new clothes. The lady in the 'Janet Roslyn' shop took quite a fancy to the handsome, dark-eyed boy Terry.

'You've got a very nice looking family,' said the lady.

'Shall I take the suit off?' said Terry, 'and keep it for best, Uncle?'

'No, you can keep it on', said Peter, 'It fits you perfectly.'

He decided, when he could afford it, to buy an extra outfit each, because their LCC clothes simply didn't fit.

'We specialize in the under twelves,' said the lady with a coy look at Uncle. What a marvellous man!

It was difficult to keep the children occupied until he could arrange for them to go to school.

It was not so much that they didn't like the country. They just weren't used to it, and were not at all clear what they were expected to do in it.

'Why don't you all go out and play in the fields?' said Peter.

All five trooped outside, to Peter's relief as he had a great deal to do. Some of the paying guests were moving out and Peter was still reorganizing the house.

His own bedroom was at the front of the house, at the end of the landing and right over the front door, chiefly because it was Aunt Georgina's opinion that this was the correct place for the owner's own room. From his window he had a view over the River Mole which was silent and filled with reeds, at the bottom of the paddock.

Peter moved his bed around three times that day in order to get the view over the Reigate Hills, extending right to Box Hill, Newlands Corner and the Hog's Back.

He was fitting up other rooms to make a flat for Anne who was helping with the cooking and looking after the tenants. Peter continued with the work, interrupted by the children's arrival, of fitting a sink unit with hot water heater and installing a cooker.

Through the window he saw the four children standing, rather lost, against the wall. John was a few feet away, carving a piece of wood out of a branch with a pen-knife.

Better go down and see what's the matter. Peter put down his tools, and went into the grounds.

'Don't you like going into the fields?' said Peter who didn't want them playing on his lawns and flowerbeds.

'It feels funny', said Babs, 'out here.'

'She's not used to it,' said Margaret. 'The Sisters didn't like us going outdoors. In case we caught cold, I suppose.'

Terry and Willy just stood there.

'You could go for a walk', said Peter.

The children stared at him.

'All right,' said Peter, 'I'll finish this job and I'll take you for a walk. We could go to the hills.'

The walk was not a success. After going about a mile, Willy sat down on the grass and refused to go any further.

The little party walked on and crossed the stile into the next field. Peter looked back. Willy was shuffling about, kicking the trunk of a huge elm tree. Then he saw them watching him, and sat down on the grass.

'Shall we go back?' Margaret said hopefully.

They all trooped back and stood looking down on the small, crumpled figure of Willy, in his new pullover and new grey shorts.

'What's the matter, Willy?'

'It's my leg,' said Willy.

'Does it hurt?'

'It aches a bit.'

'Show me where,' said Peter.

Willy looked blank.

'Uncle, Willy doesn't know where.'

'Margaret, he must know where his own leg hurts him. Show me, Willy.'

'Just all over,' Willy said.

'Funny', Peter said, 'When I handed out the sweets this morning and everyone ran for it, you were the winner.'

Margaret said, 'I'll stay with Willy and look after things for you here, Uncle.'

'No, I'll stay,' said Terry.

'An' me,' said Babs.

Peter laughed. 'That only leaves you, John, for our walk?'

John was a serious affectionate boy. 'I'll come with you, Uncle!'

Peter turned them all back towards the house. He would have to unpack his old cricket bat and stumps and get a football.

Well it was early days yet. He was eager to start teaching them the games and sports he loved.

'We're not used to it,' said Margaret, 'all this outside.'

Could it be that they were just lazy children? He hoped not. Then he reminded himself that he had not taken them for their merits and attractions.

Next Peter busied himself getting the children ready to begin school next term. For their first two weeks at Kinnersley, he kept them at home and almost every day, there was shopping.

Peter bought a new coat for Margaret; then there were satchels, hats, caps to be bought for all five children, bus passes to be obtained and so on. He had no idea how much the LCC would allow him for clothing and keep. Anyway, at present it didn't matter. He still had money left from his own savings.

Next he visited the Head Mistress of the Primary School in Crawley and the Headmaster of the Secondary School where Margaret was to go.

'I do want you to understand', said Peter to the Head Mistress, 'that I now look upon them as my children. I do sincerely hope the school will treat them as such. I mean, as typical "family" children.'

Some of the teachers were a little puzzled at his vehemence on this point.

One teacher said to the headmistress later 'He did rather go on about his family. They were to be treated as "absolutely normal" he kept saying.'

However, the children weren't quite typical at the start. For one thing, having always lived in Boarding Schools all their lives, they'd never had to get on a bus to school, or to cross a road in busy traffic during the rush hours.

So every morning Peter took them in the Land Rover to the bus-stop in Horley and stood waving goodbye until the bus disappeared from view. In the evening he waited for them again at the bus-stop to drive them home. It was better, he felt, than staying at home and worrying even if it did mean a bit of a rush later on to get tea ready and on the table for them. There was always so much to do, and yet he only had five children after all! Why, he'd always thought eight was the ideal number.

One night Terry wasn't with the children when they all got off the bus and climbed into the Land Rover.

Willy said he didn't know where Terry was. He'd waited in the playground until it was empty. No, he hadn't thought to go and ask the Headmaster or the teacher. Terry was in a different class.

'Willy, how could you be so dreamy?' Peter rarely spoke so sharply to the children, but he was anxious.

'You shouldn't upset Willy like that Uncle,' said Margaret.

Peter took a quick decision and drove them all, very fast, back to the school. There was a light in one of the classrooms and he strode in. The girl teacher sat at her desk in front of the blackboard. Terry was in the front row, writing something.

In the row that followed, Terry (who had been kept in for 'showing off') at least, appeared to be enjoying himself. He looked, with his bright face and shining, curly hair, a wholesome, attractive boy. He kept a demure face throughout.

'I must', Peter began, addressing the startled teacher, 'insist on rigid discipline regarding going to and from school.'

Peter went on to say that it was quite enough of a worry through all the stories one heard of children being waylaid, given rides, delayed for one reason or another, without the added worry of wondering where they had all got to, or by one of them being left on his or her own to come on later.

Teachers, Peter said, who kept children in after school by giving them detention when those children have journeys to make by organised public transport, should be held guilty of all subsequent events.

She was a rather young teacher. She didn't answer but just stared in some astonishment at the tall, good looking young man in front of her who talked in long sentences. She said nothing, except to nod towards the boy. 'You may go now, Terence, now your father has come for you.'

'I'm coming Uncle,' said Terence, shutting his exercise book and getting up to go. Teacher's baffled glance followed the tall man and the tiny boy. It was a glance that Peter saw and that only added to his fury and irritation.

That night he was woken by loud crying and groaning from the girls' room.

Babs was holding her head, sitting up in bed and sobbing. Margaret watched dolefully from her twin bed.

'It's her migraine', said Margaret, 'she always gets it.'

He was afraid Babs would wake the whole house, so he picked her up and carried her to his room. She was so tiny, he could have lifted her with one hand. He put her in his bed to keep her warm and then returned to collect the child's bed and carry it to his room. 'Be good', he told Margaret, 'I'll keep Babs in my room until she's better.'

He gave the child a few grains of a sedative and some water and she fell asleep. At last he lay down in his own bed. Perhaps he had been too sharp with Margaret and Babs that evening. He'd been too busy to stay with them in the bathroom until they'd finished, and when he did go in, the room seemed flooded with water. The children were paddling about and trying to swim in the bath, the soap was on the floor along with the half-soaked bath towels. He'd really let them have it. Never, never again could they take a bath without his total supervision; they could not be trusted to wash themselves without trying to drown the whole household, etc. etc. Oh, he'd rather gone on. But it was necessary. There must be rules, discipline as he'd had when he was a boy.

The trouble was, though, that he was absolutely dog-tired, yes flat out, spent . . .

Next day Miss Smith of the LCC was on the telephone. She was so pleased to hear, she said, from the CCO who'd called to see the five children that they were all doing absolutely splendidly, and could he be an angel and take two more little girls? It was rather urgent as they'd nowhere to go, so if he could help, well it would be such a wonderful favour.

So, from that day on, the family started to grow. But these two children, babies almost, he handed over to Anne. 'They're yours,' he said. 'Now you have a family too.'

10

Hopes Fade for the Grand Plan

Peter got his next two children from a church. There they were sitting in a pew of the empty Catholic Church right next door to Reigate station.

Pam, just ten years old, was very pretty with long flaxen plaits and milky skin, dressed in a red pinafore frock. Her sister Christine, age seven, was also blonde but less pretty, with short hair and looking as though she was about to burst into tears.

They were sitting in the church that day with their father who had just come off night duty at Battersea power station.

One day according to the 'Authority' the children went to live with their grandmother while their father was on night shifts, which he normally was. Later it all became too much for the grandmother. She could no longer look after the girls.

Peter heard all this over the telephone. He was to expect a call from the father when they arrived at Reigate station.

When the call came, Peter said: 'Meet me in the church. It will save you having to wait on the chilly platform and there is no other place. You can't miss it because it is next door to the station.'

It was the same church where Peter took his family of five for Mass on Sundays. He walked across to the little party sitting unmoving in the pew, staring into space.

Pam tossed back her plaits tied at each end with a scarlet bow, and smiled politely. Christine looked dejected in her brown jumper and brown pinafore dress. The father said very little as they got into the car and drove to Kinnersley.

Peter noticed that the father did not seem in any way surprised at anything he saw. Peter had been recommended by 'the Welfare' and that was enough. He did look very unhappy so Peter tried to make conversation as they went up the drive, pointing out the heifers, the dogs, the children's windows, the meadows winding down to the Mole.

He took them all up to Margaret's and Babs' room and left the father to help the girls unpack their belongings. Peter's heart was wrung with pity for the man. He thought how terrible it would be if he ever had to hand HIS children over to a stranger, as this poor man had to do! The thought upset him so much that he went back into the bedroom and said:

'Please do come and see us whenever you feel like it, whenever you have a day between shifts, there will always be a meal for you, and you will be most welcome.'

Pam smiled and smiled. Her father said wanly, 'It's very kind.' Christine clung to his hand.

Going down the big old staircase, Peter thought how strange . . . yes even Margaret, she still seems a plain, unlovable child but I couldn't bear to part with her now.

At this stage, Peter never thought to say 'no' to the Authority who kept ringing up to offer him more children. For one thing, he was still counting on the Good Women who would become the foster-mothers, when he bought more houses.

In the months that followed, children arrived by almost every telephone call, so to speak.

But Peter was not worried. He gave five of them to Anne Spence who was now living in the completely self-contained flat which Peter had now furnished, re-painted and equipped. He made the curtains and showed her how to organize and keep a budget. Meanwhile she would live rent-free and he would visit her each week and bring the housekeeping money.

Then there was another woman friend from Lourdes, Patricia, who also promised to participate in the scheme.

So the Grand Plan was beginning to shape. Soon, of course, he would have to find time to look for more houses to buy. It would all be so much easier when he had permanent women helpers to take some of the load of work off him.

He often had to do the cooking now, because Anne was too busy with her own family of five. And even when there were women to help, he still had to do the rough work like peeling seven to ten pounds of potatoes for the main meal.

Still he wasn't really worried. There was, apart from Anne, and Patricia, the tirelessly active Edith and another nice woman named Angela.

Oh, it was all going to work out beautifully, surrounded by these wonderful women to help him. Why he might even be able to keep his seven, his First Family—simply because they came first—with him in his own house wherever he might settle . . . once the Plan was in operation.

But still the Authority kept ringing up—and still the children kept coming. When Anne had as many children as she could manage, he rented for Patricia a semi-detached house in a quiet suburban road, and sent the children to her.

Was it getting a little out of hand now? Surely not. Peter felt he would soon have things organised.

His 'First Family' proved to be an intelligent bunch, and they soon, young as they were, had the measure of Uncle.

At tea-time Babs still said, even after all the months at Kinnersley:

'Please Uncle, can I take more butter?' Babs was sharp. She knew that for Uncle, the pleasure for him was in giving without stint.

Peter always put a selection of everything on the table. True, he now realized that it was not necessary to tempt their appetites but he had 'made it a rule' when he started. It was one of Peter's rules that if you made a rule and it worked, then stick to it. So the tea-table each day fairly 'groaned' under the weight. There was always a pound of fresh farm butter, peanut butter and various 'spreads' and preserves to suit all tastes, several kinds of bread, both brown and white, and pot of every flavour of jam known to the local grocer.

'Of course, you KNOW you can take more butter, Babs, if you want to,' Peter said.

'But', said Babs, 'in the convent, we got a portion and we couldn't have any more, even if we asked . . .'

'You can always have more of anything; as much as you can eat,' said Peter, 'but remember Babs, you are not to have any sugar.'

Peter was trying out a theory of his own, which was that Babs' migraine pains which were so severe that she woke him each night, were due to sugar. So Babs was forbidden to touch sugar. It was one of Uncle's rules, and that was that. After a month or so, the migraine pains began to decrease and finally stopped.

All the children showed, unconsciously, their acuteness in ASKING for things, like more butter. They quickly learned to understand this big, kind, wonderful Uncle. By asking for what he considered was theirs, they increased his pleasure in giving.

One day Margaret said: 'I wonder what happened to Linda and Denise and Kevin?'

She spoke about them on one of Peter's bad days. His bad days were those when the Authority sent a CCO who, in accordance with the law, came to 'interview' the children.

Peter disapproved of this practice. Sometimes he even hid the children or pretended he could not find them, when the Authority called.

'You know we have to do this', said the Officer.

'Yes', Peter said, 'but it's mad. What d'you expect the children to say, that I beat them every day.'

Everyone laughed uneasily.

'How can children lead normal, family lives and become ordinary children if you keep coming along to make them feel they are different?' Peter said.

However, the children were brought into Peter's study, one by one. Peter sat there smiling wryly at the conversation.

'How are you getting along?' said the Officer.

'Very well, thank you', said Babs, or Terry or Willy . . .

'And are you doing what Uncle says?' was the next question.

And so it went on. Of course, it was rather silly. But it was the law. However, Peter was always glad when the conversation took what he considered was a more 'normal' turn.

Like the question of what was going to happen to Margaret's and Babs's former friends from the convent, namely Linda, Denise and Kevin.

'They're supposed to be moving soon to a new home, much smaller,' the Officer said, 'but it's a bit uncertain as it's not built yet.'

'Well, keep us in touch,' Peter said. When the door closed behind the Officer, Margaret said:

'Couldn't Linda and Denise and Kevin come here, with us?'

'We'll see', Peter said.

The children were coming, now, rather faster than he intended. But he refused to worry about the future. Even if his women friends let him down, he could always employ a housekeeper.

It was seven all. Seven children now for Anne. That was to be her family. After all, she had a large, self-contained flat, equipped by him. And she might feel left out if he had more children than she had.

But sometimes they did have discussions about the future.

'After all,' Anne said, 'you've got your beautiful study, where you can be away from the children.'

'Yes' Peter said, 'and there's always someone in the house to look after things, with Edith coming in her holidays.' Anne said: 'And Margaret and Angela have promised to come and be "mothers" too.'

There was also Mrs. Peters, the daily.

'And there's always cook,' said Anne 'if she only stays.'

They decided they'd manage somehow.

It was not long after this conversation that things started to go wrong.

E

First Aunt Georgina decided to take her furniture and go home to the North.

Then cook who had come in reply to an advertisement in the local paper, started having hallucinations. She went about the house muttering about dark doings at the bottom of the garden. There were bodies, she said, floating in the pond. And there . . . under the full moon, she'd seen Uncle himself, dancing naked on the grass. No one, not even the last of the remaining paying guests, took any notice. However, cook's nocturnal 'visions' got worse and she finally left.

Next, Edith decided to give up the idea of becoming a 'mother' to Peter's children and became a nun instead. Off she went to France, this time for good, to join a Religious Order. Then Angela announced she was off too. Her family had moved to Canada; she's got her teaching diploma. In a short time Angela was gone too, to live and teach in Canada (where she later married and had her own children).

That still left Margaret, another friend from the Lourdes days. But she went quietly home to Yorkshire, and that left Peter alone with Anne and occasional help from Mrs. Peters. And Anne had her hands full running her own family of seven children.

As he moved about the house Peter could often hear her, through the thick old walls, disciplining her children. Her children were younger and included an infant, age two.

Fourteen children! In a great big house. This was the very condition of life from which he thought he had rescued them.

It was clearly time to sell the house and buy two separate houses, one for Anne's family, one for his.

Could he look after seven children himself? Well, he'd just have to, wouldn't he? There was no one else.

To an extent he was already reconciled to caring for the children himself. After all, he didn't know he could cook. Now he remembered the things his mother did in the kitchen and he did the same.

'From now on,' he told the children, 'you'll all have to put up with my cooking, I'm afraid.'

'That's all right, Uncle,' said Terry, 'your cooking'll be all right.'

'Roast potatoes,' Babs said, 'do lots and lots, Uncle.'

They were all so mad on roast potatoes. He set a competition once, who could eat the most. Babs ate nineteen.

The big worry really was money. He must find enough money to buy two houses. Once he did that, he was sure all the rest would come right too. Housekeepers and helps and 'mothers' would come along.

Nevertheless, he did not tell Anne that he had decided to sell Kinnersley Manor. He told himself the reason was that she loved the house. Besides who would want to buy this great old house?

Without saying anything to Anne, he went one day into Horley to have talks with the Agents about a possible sale. He asked that it should be kept confidential. No sale boards, for the present, to be put outside the house.

One day Anne saw a man walking round the garden outside the kitchen french windows. She called Peter who went out and found it was a prospective purchaser. Peter managed to show him over the whole house without 'letting on' to Anne.

He did not want to break the news to her that the time had come to part. Besides, perhaps the man was only just having a look at the house. It might all come to nothing, Peter told himself.

The Agents, however, moved quickly. One day when Peter was out, they telephoned and gave the game away. Please, they said, could they come along and erect the 'For Sale' boards at the end of the drive?

11

Peter's Dozen

Anne was tearful and distressed.

'We can't go on like this', Peter said. 'If we do, we shall reproduce almost the same situation which the children have known all their lives; a large institutional type of life in a large house run by a collection of people not their parents, all mixed up together.'

'You should have told me', said Anne, 'that you planned to sell Kinnersley'.

'It won't work,' Peter said, 'your methods are different from mine. And so they should be. I want the children to know whom they have to obey. It's better for them. I heard Margaret running to you the other day. "Auntie, save me from that horrible man".'

'Margaret adores you really,' Anne said, 'but she told me she feels you'll never like her.'

Peter found two houses in Massetts Road, Horley.

The Agents had a purchaser for Kinnersley Manor. He must repay the loan to the Bank on the sale of Kinnersley and raise a mortgage for buying the two houses.

But how? The insurance companies kept asking him what his job was. 'I have no job', Peter said. He tried explaining about the complicated business of being a father by profession, a foster-father anyway, with plans to run a big housing scheme with him as Director.

At least, he *had* a scheme, he realized with a sudden shock.

'What is your salary?' the insurance people asked.

'I have no salary', Peter said, 'I'm not in business.'

It didn't sound very promising.

He tried to be light-hearted.

'You know Anne', he said, 'my father's family crest has one word "Persevere".'

He locked himself in his study and said he wouldn't come out again without a mortgage.

It took him all day. He rang first one place, then another. Each time he patiently told his long, complicated story and was politely referred elsewhere.

Near exhaustion, he rang the Sun Life of Canada who recommended he should try Eagle Star. Was it worth it? He was near the end of his tether now . . . No, he wouldn't give in. He rang Eagle Star and asked for £6,000. They said yes, he could have it.

The two houses came to about £12,500 together, on top of which there were legal fees and the cost of moving, buying new cookers, additional household equipment, more sheets and blankets and all the other things resulting from dividing shared possessions into two completely separate lots.

It proved expensive. Yet in the end he made a profit on the sale of Kinnersley (which he'd bought for £10,000) because of all the expert conversion work he had done by himself. The price he got was £15,000. £5,000 profit!

In September 1960, Peter moved with his family of seven children into a house called Knighton Spinneys, in Massetts Road, a Victorian type house built around 1905. It stood in a tree-lined road leading from the centre of Horley. The road was full of similar houses, substantially built, solid and ugly, with enormous bay windows, high roofs, big chimneys, each with gardens and trees and a general air of homely comfort.

It was not a house he would ever have chosen for himself, but it would have to do for the time being. The Council offices were in the same road so it was no longer entirely residential, but it was convenient for shops and buses. It did have beautiful chestnut trees. Peter pointed out to the children that the houses faced a complete row of chestnuts, and he hoped it would make up for what they were losing.

The previous owner was an agent or dealer in works of

art, mostly pictures. The entire house was hung with them, all close together. When the pictures were removed, the walls had patterns all over them like noughts and crosses. So his first job was to re-paint the walls.

There were five bedrooms, one of them a single room. Peter put the four girls into one double room which was very large with a huge window. The boys had two rooms, one on each side of the landing, and Peter had the other double room which was equipped with cupboards and wardrobes. Into these he put all the children's clothes and belongings and all the things which had to be kept clean and neat, like blouses, shirts and dresses which must be hung; also pyjamas, white socks and stockings etc.

Next he collected all the girls' hairdressing equipment—combs, clips, brushes, ribbons and put it all carefully away in his own drawer, so that it would be ready to hand when he did their hair in the mornings.

He found he had enough curtains for his room and the girls' room and for the sitting-room also.

First he sat down to make sets of curtains for the boys' bedroom, bathroom and dining-room and study. He also made some curtains for Anne's new house which was called The Brambles. He made dining-room curtains for her house and then put them up for her.

Next he went out and bought new gas stoves for both houses and arranged for a second TV set. He was also shopping for new pictures, ornaments, some extra carpets, cutlery, china, kitchen utensils, cushion covers and so on.

He was hanging curtains when there was a knock at the front door. On the doorstep was Miss Winter of the LCC.

Another interview?!

'No,' said the young woman, 'I've come to ask if you would be terribly kind and take two more boys. It's very urgent.'

Peter sighed.

'Oh dear, I've got a room full of boys already. Is there no one else who could take them?'

'No, there's no one; and they've got to be moved immediately . . . it's really urgent.'

More deep sighs from Peter. Peter always coughed or
sighed when he wanted time to think.

'But I've nowhere, simply nowhere to put them,' Peter
said, playing for time.

'But they go to school in Crawley, so it'll be no trouble.
They can go with the others. And you've been so good with
the other boys from what I hear; everyone's very pleased.'

Peter realised he was being 'buttered up'. The trouble
was he rather liked it.

'All right.' More deep sighs. 'When are they coming?'

'Oh thank you, you are kind', Mrs. Winter said, 'you're
not to worry. You won't have to fetch them. I'll bring them
myself. Today then, after school.'

Peter went out and bought two double bunks, for £25
each. Actually it made more floor space.

Brian aged nine and his brother Paul, 11, moved in with
Willy and Terry. John, rather a loner among the children
because he was at 13 so much older, was quite happy to
be moved downstairs. Peter heard him that evening sawing
away at some wooden shelves. John, he thought, was the
only one like himself with any aptitude for using his hands.

The newcomers were introduced at tea and made a good
impression. Brian was a sturdy, good looking boy; he looked
happy too, rather cheeky. Paul was also attractive with a
nice smile, but quieter. He had a habit of saying 'Thanks,
I don't mind'.

However, they soon entered into the spirit of it. That is
to say, this was no ordinary suburban home—'We're not
Bohemians exactly,' Peter told the newcomers, 'but we're
different!'

Paul and Brian weren't saying anything. They kept their
eyes on their plates. Peter always cut mountains of bread
slices for tea. He took his seat at the top of the table and
then, after Grace was said, he started throwing the slices
one at a time at each child.

'You see the idea?' Peter said to the newcomers. 'Each slice must land directly on to each plate. Anyway it saves all that business of handing the bread round.'

At that point, the telephone rang. It was someone from the LCC to say that they'd all be delighted at Knighton Spinneys to hear the news. Uncle was to have three more children to add to his family. Quite soon . . .

They were referring to Uncle's recent query into the fate of three children of one family, named Linda, Denise and Kevin who had been convent inmates with Margaret and Babs. Well, Uncle and the children would be pleased to hear that the Authority had now decided that instead of going to a new Home, not yet built, they could come to Knighton Spinneys instead.

You see, said the Officer from the LCC, the new Home was not going to be built after all.

Uncle and the children—the only photograph taken of the whole
family together. *From top to bottom*, John (15), Margaret (13),
Paul (12), Babs (11), Pam (11), Linda (10), Terry (10), Brian (9),
Denise (9), Willy (8), Christine (8) and Kevin (7)

A walk in Wales

Time for tea

Some of the happiest times of the children's childhood were spent
in Wales. Here are ten of them—with Uncle.
Left to right: Linda, Brian, Kevin, Willy, Denise, Pam, Christine,
John, Paul, Babs

PART TWO

Peter Flees with the Children

12

Trouble

Now Peter had his own family of twelve. He was exhausted but reconciled to it. He took over all the cooking as well as the housework. His days were full. He watched television with the children in the evenings, and longed for eight o'clock when he could put all twelve to bed and sit and rest.

His peace was suddenly shattered. Rumours were spreading through the little country town. What, exactly, was happening at Knighton Spinneys? It was 'disgusting' that twelve small children, six girls and six boys, were living alone with a young man. Why was there no woman in the house?

Not that anyone dared to say these things to Peter himself. Instead they complained to Father Woolmer. After all, it was the future of his flock that was at stake.

Poor Father Woolmer, limping with arthritis, moved lamely about, wondering what to do.

One day he telephoned Denis Allen at the LCC Children's Department, begging for help in the present explosive situation.

Denis took the train to Horley and went to the Presbytery to see the priest.

'I've tried', Father Woolmer said, 'to talk to Peter about it, about all these horrible rumours shooting around.'

'What does Jeffcock say about it?' Denis asked.

'He just says . . . "Uhu, let them think what they like!" '

After some consultation, it was agreed that Denis should telephone Peter's mother and ask her if she had also heard the rumours.

Yes, she had, she told Denis Allen. It was all very worrying.

'Worrying? You mean you are not happy about Peter?' Denis asked.

No, she was anxious only about the rumours. She and

Peter's sister Pamela knew that Peter was doing a wonderful job; he was doing what he'd always wanted to do, that was to give a real family life back to children who had lost theirs. But was it wise? That was the thing. They felt it was unwise for it to continue like this, without a woman in the house.

Denis felt reasonably satisfied with this telephone interview. The conversation was entirely honest and outspoken. He felt relieved that there had been no attempt to pretend that the rumours did not exist. He was therefore over the first hurdle.

Heartened by this, he went to see Peter, and said it would be wiser if Peter employed a woman in the house, simply to cover himself against all the stupid rumour-mongering.

Anne Spence told Denis: 'I'd like to know where all the women are who could look after children so beautifully as Peter does. It's like that ghastly experience years ago when rumours were made against him. He wanted to help children and he wasn't going to let any silly woman stop him.'

'You say he's unwise!'

'Of course, it was unwise. If it happened to me . . . a thing like that; I'd say, well that's my lot!'

Denis Allen said, 'Yes I know, I agree.'

Anne rushed on:—'You know about it then? You know what happened? That whole experience broke him down in health. To think people could even think things like that. But this is why I admire Peter so much. In spite of this woman who created a scandal, probably due to her own frustrations because she couldn't get what she wanted . . . it takes a long time to forget a thing like that. And it took enormous courage for him to go on. But he did go on.'

There was a pause. Denis watched Anne's face. She went on, more quietly now.

'Peter has a gift for children and a gift for home-making. Just because he can do all these wonderful things—often much, much better than I can do for instance; I don't sew like he does . . . why should people think him a rotter? They might call him names, but how can they really have any doubts about him?'

So Peter gave in; at least for the present. He tried to make the best of it. A Mrs. Coughlan, with her husband and three children, moved into Peter's house from their small farmhouse.

He had only one room to give the whole family but he gave up his study for their use, thus enabling them to have a "flat" of two rooms. Mrs. Coughlan helped him with some of the work. He and Mrs. Coughlan now often sat down together at the kitchen table, between jobs, and drank endless cups of tea. 'Like two gossiping housewives,' Peter said. Now he had no room of his own away from the children, he did his correspondence in the kitchen.

Instead of the cosy family life he had dreamed of, there were now 18 people squashed together in this house called Knighton Spinneys. He'd wanted a natural, simple family household just as other people had, his friends and neighbours. Why did everyone try to stop him? Why didn't they leave him in peace?

He didn't admit to himself that deep down, perhaps unconsciously at this stage, he was already planning flight.

There was nothing he could do about it at the moment.

It was shortly after this that the kindly and charitable body, the local branch of the Round Table, which is a branch of Rotary, a business man's social and charitable organisation, asked if they could do anything to help Peter with his good work.

Peter said politely, 'No thank you.' He was grateful to them for their kindness and goodwill but this was just what he did NOT want. To accept help from an organisation would give that 'institutional' touch to things which he hated.

He was encouraged, nevertheless, by their gesture. 'At least', he said to Anne when he called at her house one day, 'the MEN of this town don't look upon us as freaks. THEY don't come to our door asking silly questions. Not like some of the dear, good ladies, guardians of the social scene who keep asking you "why these nice little girls have no woman to look after them!" '

It was in the Knighton Spinneys house that Peter started to teach the children to do some of the things he'd loved doing as a boy.

He taught all the girls to knit. Terry was the only one of the boys who wanted to knit too.

Peter gathered the children round him to teach them. It was relaxing to sit like this in a low-seated armchair. Caring for them, washing them in the mornings, seeing they brushed their teeth, brushing their hair made his back ache a bit from bending. Now if they stood by his chair and watched him knit, they did not have to strain their necks just to see his face.

'Now,' Peter said, 'are you all watching?' It was not for nothing he'd been able to knit himself a heavy polo-neck sweater when he was a small boy.

Terry was eager. 'Uncle, I think I can do it; let me.'

'Now do you want to try Willy?'

Willy shrugged. He was a remote, rather silent child, something of a day-dreamer. Whereas Terry, Peter thought, was sometimes a little too eager to please.

Everyone knitted away so the room was full of the clatter of knitting-needles, but Pam and Babs soon got bored. They wanted to go out to the shed at the top of the garden to feed the heifer, which was the last one from the six Peter had kept at Kinnersley.

The girls ran off to do their favourite chore, feeding, watering, brushing and petting the heifer.

There was another 'pet' from the Kinnersley days. It was a charming hen which Peter gave to Terry because he loved it the most. Terry fed his own jam sandwiches to the hen and let the hen sip from his cup of tea. It was a pretty china cup too. Peter loved pretty china.

Terry and Willy had their own tortoises which they'd brought from the Kinnersley house. This created a constant panic in the family because the tortoises could travel with amazing speed and were always getting lost.

Linda and Denise also had a tortoise each which Peter bought for them. He also bought a golden retriever puppy called Judy with a smooth, silky coat and fat tummy and curly tail. Judy was a sensation on the day Peter brought her home. He'd intended her for his own pet.

'All right,' Peter said, 'stop shouting, all of you, you can all share her.'

So Judy got fatter than ever. She had cornflakes for breakfast along with the children, every morning before school. Only she tended to get twelve separate portions. The children trained her to jump on to a seat the other side of the kitchen partition and beg for it through a window in the partition.

Two ducks which Peter bought were given to John. John made a small house for them, dug a short ditch, concreted it, filled it with water and the ducks lived there happily for a year. Though at times, the water did come through the concrete.

'Don't worry, John,' Peter said, 'I thought you made a very fine job of that concrete, old man.'

Terry came running in one day screaming 'Uncle, oh Uncle! Come quickly!' Everyone rushed out. There was Terry's pet hen lying, apparently dead, near the Land Rover.

'Uncle do something' Terry shouted.

Peter bent down. 'Sad and sudden end. Sorry Terry.'

Terry was in tears. He said his pet hen had somehow got on to the seat of the Land Rover. When he arrived, she seemed to fall, hitting her head on a large bolt on the floor.

Christine, the 'emotional' one of Peter's family started to weep too. Whether for the pet hen or for Terry's tragic loss, was not quite clear.

'Look children,' said Peter, 'keep calm. I'm going to bring everyone a pet today. When you get home from school . . . well, you'll see.'

Pam was radiant. 'Uncle, you really mean it?'

Of all the children Pam was the most devoted to animals.

Peter bought her an Abyssinian guinea pig. After that Pam took the guinea pig with her everywhere, cradling the little pig in her arms. With her long golden hair she looked a perfect 'Alice'.

From the pets he brought home that day, Pam was given several hamsters. She always kept at least one hamster and the guinea pig near her bed at night.

Until Linda complained she couldn't sleep because the hamster's spinning wheel made so much noise, so they were transferred to the bathroom at night.

Margaret kept a tortoise, a rabbit and a guinea pig; Denise felt very proud when *her* guinea pig had babies. Terry was given two chickens and two Chinese geese as well as two kittens to make up for the loss of his beloved hen. Terry and Christine had hedgehogs. Babs had a rabbit.

In the end there were so many pets that Peter had to build a wire-netting run and the whole lot were put into it together; two chickens, two rabbits, the hedgehogs, two kittens etc. Also the ducks were put there from time to time because they kept digging up the lawn, or rather what was left of the lawn after twelve children had played on it for a few months.

All the animals lived happily together and managed to find the food they preferred from among the assorted stuff which the children fed to them.

Then one day, rats killed everyone's pet tortoise. They were found scattered over the garden, dead.

It made an emotion-charged day.

Terry said: 'Uncle, it's our fault. If we'd brought them indoors for the winter—'

Pam wouldn't eat any tea. Neither would Linda. Later Christine was sick.

Peter said 'All right, that settles it. No more tortoises—ever.'

Into the attic Peter put a model railway. The long swing ladder from the landing was pulled down and the children climbed up to play with the railway. Peter made it a rule they could not climb up unless he was there to supervise.

The floor of the attic was boarded, flat and strong. It made an ideal place. Peter bought dozens of O-Gauge lines, fixed them to the floor and allotted each 'railwayman' his own space on the floor, so that each had a 'section'. Over the whole layout, several trains ran quite separately so that those children who were really keen, had their own seats, with engine trucks or carriages. The original 'railwaymen' were John, Terry, Willy and Brian.

John loved the railway the most and as usual, was the most enterprising, so that his section was said to be right up to the Great Western standard. But the most interested onlooker was Linda, who soon had to be given her own 'section'.

She loved all games, especially those one could play lying on the floor.

Peter often called to Terry and Willy:

'Would you like to come upstairs and we'll play with the railway?'

'No thank you Uncle, we're watching television.'

But he was disappointed that only John and Linda seemed to take a real interest in the model railway he had installed with such loving care.

'I thought with such a big track as ours, you'd all be thrilled with it,' Peter said sadly.

'It's really your game,' said Willy truthfully, 'you're best at it. You and John.'

Still they had other games, including a dart board, racing demon, pontoon and they all liked Peter's favourite game of Monopoly, which he really enjoyed most of all, until one day Margaret beat him at it.

Peter hoarded all these special family occasions, like Margaret beating him while Linda played with her Lego game on the floor, building houses and castles or took out her dolls to dress and undress them. This was what he meant by real family life.

It was difficult to believe that Mrs. Coughlan and her family lived in the house as they were very quiet and never interfered.

F

Peter liked watching television with the children too. So much so that at first the children were allowed to eat their bread and jam and take their tea in front of the TV set.

Until the carpet became patterned with jam stains, and Peter made special times for viewing. There was always a Children's Hour programme while all 13 watched together. Peter called it family viewing and found it restful.

So their daily programme after school was homework, children's television, followed by high tea, an hour or so of playtime in the sitting-room or garden. Then Peter started getting them to bed. After eight o'clock the no-talking rule began.

A new problem was Christine who followed forlornly where the other children led, but was still nervous and absent-minded. Also she wet her bed. Before going to his own bed each night, Peter went in to see her and finding her bed damp, removed the blankets and replaced them. The habit continued until he moved her bed into his own room for about a month. Then she was cured, just as Babs had lost her migraine. In this way Peter learned that each child's need was to be singled out for special, individual treatment. It was still a novelty for them to be noticed as individuals instead of one of a large, massed group of children.

For a time Christine needed him most and so Christine became a favourite and remained so. Peter was not only learning now to understand the children; he was also learning about himself.

13

Sewing and Cinema

Peter was not pleased when at last the local press turned up for a story. Here he was trying to bring them up as normal kids, just like the kids-next-door, but no one would let him.

He didn't know how the story had leaked to the press. Though it was clear, when they wanted him to pose for a photograph doing his chores, that someone had already noticed that the 12 children of that wife-less man in Horley were impeccably dressed.

'Yes, I am the seamstress in the household,' said Peter, 'but is that really a story for you?'

That day when the children arrived home from school at 4.30, they joined in the interview, and quite enjoyed the sight of their Uncle being haplessly grilled; especially about his sewing. Peter had tried without success, so far, to teach the girls how to sew on buttons.

'Buttons are the worst problem,' Peter said, wincing as the camera was turned in his direction while he sat with needle and thread.

'Really . . . do you have to do this? I mean, I must look an absolute idiot looking as though I can't find the button-hole.'

'Just hold it', the cameraman said, 'children keep back.'

Peter rattled on, to cover his embarrassment.

'As a matter of fact, I don't really have much mending to do; clothes are well-made nowadays and in most cases, if manufacturers use good cotton when making them up, they'll last as long as they need.'

'Buttons are the worst problem . . . I say how long have I got to go on sitting here like an idiot? . . . oh all right then . . .'

'Won't be long now,' said the cameraman.

'Buttons wear the thread', Peter mumbled. 'I'm always having to sew buttons on.'

'Really—it's fascinating,' said the reporter.

'Skirt hems are difficult too. I must have taken one up or let one down at least once a week this year.'

'The swank thing is to sew a hem by hand! It's not too difficult on a wool skirt or a Terylene school skirt; but with shimmering nylon or acrilan pastel-coloured summer things . . .!'

'Do go on, Mr. Jeffcock, it's so interesting,' the reporter said.

'Do you like your work?' Margaret asked him (the reporter).

'Tell me,' the reporter said, 'how does he treat you, your Uncle?'

'Not too bad,' said Margaret.

'He's all right,' this from Willy.

'Could do worse, you know,' from Babs.

'Can he cook . . . does he feed you properly?'

'If you're not gone soon,' Peter said, 'they'll get nothing. And it's liver and onions and roast potatoes!'

Howls of delight from the children ended the interview. Peter was still wondering whether he ought to have kicked the newspaperman off the doorstep. Ah well, it was no harm. It might make a lot of ladies think about looking after some children as well!

But he resolved; never again. He felt it was bad for the children, and he could see that Paul was upset by it.

Paul had disappeared when he learned what was going on in the sitting-room. He didn't care for publicity.

Paul was an attractive personality with a certain reserve. Peter understood exactly how Paul felt. He sympathized. Paul, he felt, had never asked to live with him and therefore felt no obligation towards him. Paul had to feel free and entitled to reject Peter and the whole outfit and Peter felt that this was a perfectly justifiable point of view.

Peter decided to take the children to the cinema that Bank Holiday week. It was still a rare excitement for at least seven of the children who had only been once during their convent lives.

He enjoyed going with them; it was fun noticing the astonishment of the girl at the cash-desk and the man who took the tickets. Also it was a rest from the incessant chatter and conversation as long as Margaret didn't start giving her comments as she often did. Did these 12 children really talk more continuously and noisily than other children or was it just that he had never lived as long with children before?

Peter had to prod two of the children 'on duty' that day to help him clear the table. It was their turn to do this but none of the children were eager to help, except perhaps Linda.

Linda seemed to be the only one of the children who, at that time, showed a motherly interest in HIM, and how *he* felt. To the others, it seemed, he was just 'that man' or 'only Uncle'.

'Are you tired Uncle?' Linda said, 'I'll help you.'

Peter was convinced she was the most kind-hearted of the children and for this reason he inclined to make a favourite of her. Peter knew that all children who lose their homes— some have none to lose from the start—are disturbed and sometimes 'difficult'. Linda was neither and, quite unaccountably, level-headed.

Babs said she'd eaten too many roast potatoes and couldn't move. As it was a Bank Holiday, Peter cooked their favourite weekend meal of two large legs of roast mutton, served with roast potatoes, tinned peas and a pint and a half of thick, dark gravy which took him 20 minutes to prepare. The children stood round the stove watching while he mixed it from sliced onions, lard, butter, cornflour, mustard, herbs, cream, seasoning and olive oil and water. After this there was a bowl of tinned fruit from two very large tins served with Ideal milk which the children preferred to real cream.

They all set off for the cinema on foot—ten minutes walk. However, when they reached the cinema it was found there

were no half-price tickets that day because of the holiday.
Peter hesitated. He was spending more than £12 a week on
food alone now and money was getting short. If he bought
13 adult-priced tickets now, it would be very nearly the
price of the evening meal he planned to give them next day,
which was to have a basis of omelettes requiring two dozen
eggs.

'What's the matter Uncle, can't we go in?' Margaret said.
Margaret always anticipated some disaster or disappointment.

'I'll have a word with the Manager,' Peter said.

The Manager was adamant.

'No exceptions', he said stridently. 'Full price today or
nothing.'

They all trooped home sadly.

It was a relief to get back to Knighton Spinneys that day
and switch on the television and its holiday programme.
Peter wondered how parents managed before it was invented.

Peter loved what he called the 'modern classical' as well
as film and stage musicals, and all the Elvis Presley songs.
He thought it was odd that he knew far more about the
emerging pop sounds of the early 60s than any of the
children.

He kept adding to his pre-war collection of Tannhauser,
Gounod's Faust, and Paul Robeson songs by buying all the
Supremes and the first 'Bee Gees'. It was he who led the
Beatles fashion and listened to all their songs on radio with
even more enthusiasm than the children showed. He bought
as many long-playing records as he could, like Oklahoma
and Oliver and on Sundays and holidays, the record-player
played throughout the day. He switched on the radio when
he rose at seven and he liked light music or pop to sound out
above the usual breakfast din throughout the meal.

Peter held some vague notion that all this musical intake
must be good for the children in some way, though he was too
honest a man to deny that he enjoyed it too. So when Willy
one day remarked 'that's a good tune Uncle, what is it?'

during The Marriage of Figaro, Peter felt that perhaps after all, his efforts to interest the children in music might be bearing fruit.

Babs was fond of drawing and liked making sketches in charcoal of enormous ladies with grotesque faces, huge black eyes and masses of black hair. She did this for hours on end, her own red silky hair hanging over her freckled cheeky face. She filled a dozen half-crown books with her ladies' gallery.

Pam and Christine liked doing water-colouring. They also filled books with them. Pam, Christine and Babs spread their books out on the floor and Peter let them keep a pot of water on the carpet, a large, solid pot that would not tip over.

Next day it was business as usual. Peter rose at seven and went downstairs to make himself a pot of tea which he always took back to his bedroom to let it brew. Meanwhile he went round every bedroom, drawing the curtains and waking each child individually if still asleep.

No time for morning kisses. Occasionally he had to strip the sheets and blankets right off Paul who never moved until the last minute.

A blast of noise began as the children, woken by him according to his rule, released the pent-up conversation forbidden earlier.

'Uncle,' said Denise, 'why do you have this rule about silence in the early morning before you wake us?' Denise was a tiny girl with the same smooth, brown hair of her older sister Linda.

'Because', Peter said, 'I can remember so many other people's houses where children were allowed to disturb the entire household, by talking, running to and from the bathroom etc., without any thought whatsoever for Daddy who needed his night's sleep, for Mummy who did not want to get up before time every morning . . . all because some rather selfish little children, necessarily sent to bed before their parents, for the good of their own health, were alert and wide eyed and full of fun too early, just because—'

'Please Uncle,' Babs interrupted. Babs did not like long sentences and was quickly and easily bored. 'Uncle . . . tonight is Treasure Island . . . can we have tea in front of the television like we used to do at Kinnersley, please Uncle.'

'Oh Uncle, can we?'

Daily routine for Peter and the children was now more or less regulated by the viewing-times, and the rhythmic order of this was not merely acceptable but even soothing to Peter. It reminded him of his life at home as a boy, with Children's Hour on radio from five to six o'clock in the evening.

14

Housewife's Choice

The whole of that year and right up to Whitsuntide of the next, Mrs. Coughlan and her family, occupying two rooms of Knighton Spinneys, tactfully kept to their quarters. There was little or no contact between the two families, except when the children were at school when Mrs. Coughlan sometimes emerged for a cup of tea and a gossip. She also offered to help Peter with the washing and ironing.

So, outwardly at least, the conventions and feelings of local people were respected. No one could any longer point a finger. Or say, 'that house' with all those children and no woman in it, even though the children never saw the woman, except on odd occasions.

Peter kept to an immaculate routine. If it was Clean Clothes Day, he saw to it that these were ready the night before. Shoes all cleaned and breakfast laid. Biggest problem was sharing the bathroom. While they took this in turns, Peter went downstairs, made the tea and put out the milk for cereals. There were always eight different cereals on the table, plus as much milk as they wanted, and tea. Peter did not believe in Cooked Breakfast.

'All you need at breakfast is good quality bulk. Protein may well be concentrated but it leaves you empty very soon.'

This was his maxim, and it seemed to work. Everyone was healthy.

Once breakfast had started, Peter went upstairs to collect the girls whose hair needed doing each morning.

He brushed and combed each one, arranging it in turns so that Pam and Christine could first have their breakfast and then come to him for their plaits to be done.

Pam's hair was very long, very flaxen and so thick that the plaits took some holding together. However, those great, thick-fingered hands were skilled now at tying the plaits with ribbons at the ends, or sometimes tying the ribbons on her head so that she could have a change of style. No wonder people stared at the pretty schoolgirl who looked like a shining doll with her neat head and figure. Pam always looked just as perfect when she came home in the afternoons, and she was complacently aware of this.

He gave Christine a different style because her hair was short.

She was almost plain compared to her sister Pam but he loved her for her humility. She was quiet and spoke little.

'Stand quite still; I mustn't break your hair; it's so fine but it's growing nicely now. No, it's too thin for plaits; shall we try tying it back with a bow? No, it doesn't suit her, does it Pam?'

Peter secured Christine's hair with ribbons high on her head, letting her golden hair fall in soft folds round her puckish face.

'Don't forget, Christine darling, you have to start writing lessons with Auntie Pamela next week. Reading and writing. Won't that be lovely? In a classroom all by yourself.'

'Yes, Uncle,' said Christine.

'You will like being Auntie Pamela's pupil, won't you?'

'Oh yes, Uncle,' said Christine. After a long pause, she added in a whisper, 'She's very nice.'

It was quite a long speech for Christine. She suffered not from lack of intelligence but more from a crushing shyness and lack of self-confidence. Christine's mother had died in childbirth after having Christine. She always listened obediently to her splendid sister Pam and followed her about whenever Pam let her.

After breakfast, Peter walked the whole family to the bus stop.

The only child who required little supervision was John who at 14 years of age was able to lend a hand with the larger jobs. John was also the only one who made his bed without being told to do so. The boy was quiet and undemanding. Peter told himself it was because John was older, well almost grown-up, that he gave the boy less attention than he gave to the others. But he was more patient with John. One of his pleasures was showing John how to paint and do carpentry and make things. At school John was still behind with his studies. It worried Peter. Perhaps he was too 'ambitious' for his 'first child', he thought.

As soon as he had waved them goodbye on the bus, Peter returned to the house and turned up the radio in the kitchen.

He timed himself that he must do all the necessary jobs between the start and the end of Housewife's Choice. In fact he looked forward to it, especially if his favourite Frank Sinatra or Dean Martin records were played. He thought he might ask Linda to write to the BBC and ask for Sinatra's latest number to be played. It would be good handwriting and spelling practice for her. For three months he had taught the first five children while they waited to get places in school. After all, his mother had taught him at home herself until he was nearly ten years old.

First he cleared the table, swept the floor and removed everything to the kitchen where all the washing-up of the previous 24 hours was to be done during Housewife's Choice. Of course, this system meant having extra china, extra cups and saucers especially, and he liked nice china! Peter was sure that this once-a-day washing-up was ideal and wondered why no one seemed to have thought of it before.

It did make a considerable pile but everything was neatly stacked as though on top of a shop counter. Also it meant that he could give more time to the children instead of disappearing into the kitchen to wash up after every meal. Except on holidays when he recruited some of them to help.

Housewife's Choice ended and on the dot, Peter left the kitchen to tackle the bedrooms. Peter disliked unmade beds, having seen so many on his visits all over the country long ago, at the time when he was involved in property and had to visit people to check repairs or rebuilding.

After bedroom tidying (why did all children always leave their belongings lying about on the floor—books, comics, toffee papers, pencils, pyjamas, towels?), Peter cleaned out the sitting-room, swept the floors with either broom or vacuum-cleaner, cleaned round the bathroom, wiping up remains of spilled toothpaste, soap and water. It took some time to sort out the clothing on Clean Clothes Day and to decide which garment belonged to which child. Then he put the items away into the appropriate drawers, cupboards and shelves.

Then came a break for coffee. Sometimes he took this by visiting Anne to see how her family were getting along. She had nine children now.

'Why is it', Peter asked her, 'that not one of my boys will make their beds? Why is it?'

'Every single one of my children make their beds,' said Anne.

'And why is it?' Peter went on, 'that none of my children will look after their own clothes and possessions, not even their toys. Everything's left on the floor for me to pick up.'

'All my children are tidy,' said Anne.

'Can you explain it?' said Peter.

'I simply insist that my children make their beds. You are to soft.'

'Well I suppose so. But I *do* want them to grow to be strong characters!'

Peter went into the shopping-centre to get food for the day's meals.

He thought about what Anne had said. He knew that she was firm with the children when necessary, but then so was he, wasn't he? Look at the way he'd lashed out at Paul and Willy yesterday for being rude and cheeky.

Of course, he couldn't give more than a tiny slap. With his strength that was enough!

The children had called him names. It wasn't the first time either; all because he warned them to make their beds and to tidy up. He knew, of course, that they regretted it immediately. It was just that they had terrible tempers, some of them. It was understandable. They must have suffered terribly as infants. He knew he couldn't ever make it up to them for the loss of a mother, no matter how hard he tried.

Some of the children hadn't spoken to him at breakfast. Well, they'd soon come round. There were birthdays coming up soon. Seven birthdays between September and Christmas! He must remember to buy some new cake tins and equipment for icing the birthday cakes as well as tiny birthday cake candles. Now, how many would he need this time?

Peter started early to get the tea ready. There were ten pounds of potatoes to peel. He might make a big spaghetti dish with mince, but there had to be roast potatoes, so he got out his largest pans and dishes. He must be ready by about 4.15 p.m. when they returned from school and he must have a big fire burning then, so that it all looked cosy with a tempting odour coming from the kitchen. It was one of his rules that he never allowed them to come home to an empty house. He didn't know how working mothers could do it?

This thought sent Peter into a long reverie about the contemporary industrial system and its demands on female labour, with consequent hardships for the children etc. Peter wondered sometimes if perhaps he ought to have gone in for politics. Well, it was too late now. He could hear the conversation of 12 children coming up the garden path.

It was another of his rules that they must first hang up their coats and satchels, change their shoes and then go upstairs to change out of their school uniforms. Only then could they come downstairs and wait for the children's television programme to begin.

Having got everything ready, Peter was able to sit and watch it with them. He made it a rule always to do this. He felt that the quality of the programme was less important than the fact that they were all watching it together. So everyone watched, sitting side by side, except for Linda who preferred to play with her doll's house or ludo and was given a special part on the floor to do it on.

It was also a rule that no one should talk while the programme lasted, not even Peter himself. He explained to the children that talking and watching were incompatible and with this they agreed.

When the children's programme was over, Peter went to the kitchen to make tea. He carried the dishes himself to the table. Even John wasn't big and strong enough to help with that. Most of the pans and dishes he used were large enough to take a fair-sized turkey.

After tea, two of the children helped him to clear the table; they took it in turns each evening. He stacked everything tidily, swept the floor and did his evening jobs, like preparing for the morning, including shoe-cleaning and making sure there would be no last-minute hitch in the next morning rush. All 12 must be on time to catch that bus. John helped with the shoes so that he could go upstairs and wash Christine's hair. At eight o'clock everyone went to bed except for two who were allowed to have a 'late night' in his company.

Everyone said prayers before getting into bed. Peter seated them all 12 on the stairs, row upon row of them and made them say the Rosary either before tea or after. They filled the stairway from top step to bottom, facing the Statue of Our Lady (who gave the Rosary into the hands of St. Dominic), standing in the hall.

'Holy Mary', began Margaret and then remembered something. 'Can I make a cake tonight, please Uncle?'

15

Peter Wins a Prize

The point about cooking for children is that once you have
set a standard, it has to be maintained. So that even if you
started off an indifferent or unpractised cook, you may—
after cooking daily for 12 appreciative children—end up a
superb one.

This soon happened to Peter who, if the truth were ad-
mitted, wasn't half-bad when he started. He had never
actually cooked anything before but he had watched his
mother do it 30 years before.

Peter let himself be persuaded to enter a local cakemaking
competition. A fruit cake. It had to be made at home and
then submitted for judgment. To nobody's surprise except
Peter's, he won easily.

It caused the usual talk and gossip. This was nothing new
for Peter either, but this time the gossip was of different order.
People were beginning at last to accept that Peter was no
ordinary man, that he could do things that other people
couldn't do. So there was no spiteful talk about Peter and
the children this time, as news of the fruit cake competition
swept around the neighbourhood. Except that some women
said that a man could have and probably did have, an unfair
advantage because of his stronger wrists which helped with
beating butter and sugar to a cream. Luckily, few people
knew that in this respect too, Peter was a man with no
ordinary wrists!

The children were delighted. They were accustomed to
being stopped by strangers or asked at school 'can he cook?'
. . . or 'does he feed you properly?' . . . Now the reply
came pat and proud:

'He's a marvellous cook! Didn't you know he won a
competition for it?' Willy, especially, went round repeating
this. Willy often got into fights at school, on account of

Uncle. More than once he returned home with a black eye. Someone had 'attacked' Uncle, Willy always said.

Success in the local competition entitled Peter to enter the next round. This time it was a Victoria Sandwich. Peter decided to have a go.

'I've never ever made one before', Peter said, 'I've never even heard of one. I've made sponge cakes and sandwich cakes but never a Victoria one.'

'Oh go on Uncle,' said Linda and Margaret, 'you can get the recipe and you'll win, you know you will.'

So Peter mixed and beat and creamed with that seemingly effortless but powerful precision of his.

When it was ready, all the children crowded round the excellent gas-fired oven with the glass door, as Peter carefully took it out and laid it carefully on a wind-protected table and stood back to regard it.

'Super,' said Willy.

'Yum yum,' said Terry.

'Oh Uncle you are clever,' the girls all said.

Even John who was always good with his hands, was duly impressed, and the more sophisticated children Paul and Brian and Pam looked on with friendly encouragement.

The whole family piled into the Land Rover to rush it to the same shop where the first round of the competition was conducted. However, Peter's Victoria Sandwich proved to be the only entry this time as it represented the district rather than the town entry.

'It's really just for fun,' Peter said as they climbed back into the overloaded car once more. 'Honestly, children, you needn't all look so deadly serious as though the honour of our household is at stake.'

'Oh, but it is Uncle, dearest Uncle darling,' Margaret said with, for her, an unusual fervour.

Peter realized that for the moment he was something of a hero in Margaret's eyes. More than two years of living with Margaret had begun already to alter his first opinion of the child. He still thought her an awkward and argumentative child but she was his now and it made a difference. He tried to give her self-confidence and to calm her fierce temper. He understood only too well that life was a struggle for her. She was too intelligent not to be conscious of the contrast between herself and the pretty, self-assured Pam whom she always tried to avoid as far as possible. Margaret was looking almost pretty now. Uncle had thrown away her metal-rimmed N.H.S. spectacles and bought smart new ones. Also her squint had been corrected by a muscle operation at Westminster Hospital.

'You won't call me that,' Peter said, pleased with her, 'if I don't win this time.'

'You will . . . you will,' they all shouted.

It was not long afterwards that the cake-shop announced the winner of the district competition. Peter had won again.

The children were so excited by the fame that all this brought to Knighton Spinneys that when the next competition was announced, they urged him to enter.

This competition was for Home Baking and was sponsored by the Gas Board and McDougall's Flour, together with the Egg Marketing Board. It was an annual affair, restricted to amateurs. Anyone who cooked, or taught cooking professionally, and was not a 'home' cook, was not eligible. However, this did not exclude people who had done such work in the past, who perhaps had married and were now cooking for their own families at home. Therefore the standard was potentially very high. It was open to all-comers of any age in the United Kingdom.

Peter felt rather nervous this time, having entered the competition under the title 'Mrs.' and realizing that now he was going to be found out!

The third round was to be held at the Gas Board's area Headquarters. When the day came, Peter knew he could not face going there alone. He asked Linda to go with him because she was the most confident and relaxed of all the children. When they arrived, permission was granted for Linda to enter the room where the competition was held.

She was the only child present. No one seemed to mind that he was not a woman, but he was conscious of some interested glances in his direction and Linda's.

'Uncle dear, there's no need to be nervous,' Linda said, clutching his hand tightly. They sat together in the long, narrow waiting-room until the instructions were given. There were eight district winners involved this time and they were to compete in two rounds of four at a time. The Winner would be selected by the Judges after both rounds were completed and this would be calculated by the number of points awarded to each.

Peter and Linda looked at the four Gas cookers provided at the tables, the sets of identical bowls, spoons, knives, weighing scales etc. and the Invigilator watching each table.

'Look Uncle, those ladies are the Judges.'

'I wish we hadn't come,' Peter said.

'Pull yourself together Uncle,' Linda said.

When his turn came, Linda helped him on with the apron. Instead of the frilly aprons worn by the lady competitors, a masculine butcher's type apron was thoughtfully provided for Peter.

Peter made Linda stand in front of him the whole time, to give him confidence, so that he could pretend he was just cooking at home for her and all the children.

Peter approached his table where he was to make, this time, Swiss Roll . . . positioned Linda in front of him, and waited for the Starter to drop the flag for the 'off'.

Peter kept his eyes on his table—a quick look to see that the stove was switched on and he started mixing the butter and sugar exactly as he always did at home. He always spent a long time on the creaming process, just as his mother had done.

Now, as he worked, he recognized that he was copying exactly every gesture and movement his mother made in that far-off kitchen of his childhood. He knew how she held the bowl, the angle at which she stood, the speed for each action and for him now, it was instinctive. He knew he had to beat the mixture until it was a light creamy colour so that it should become absolutely, indivisibly, one ingredient and therefore in a condition to receive any others added, and to coat them and blend them with them so finely that the whole should be a delicate mass of fine ingredients blended together beyond all possible recognition.

Now he did it all again, just as he had shown Margaret and Pam and Linda dozens of times.

He noticed that the other competitors had put their mixture in the oven, but he went on beating, feeling no panic and even managed a smile for Linda who stood there like a statue.

When he felt sure the mixture could not possibly be improved upon, he mixed in the remainder, poured it into the pan and popped it into the oven.

Meanwhile one by one, the other ladies removed their pans from the ovens and emptied them on to the grease-proof paper and like lightning spread the jam, and rolled them up, placing their completed Swiss Roll carefully to one side, as instructed. Then they stood stiffly, as though on parade.

Peter was the last of all to roll his Roll and to put in the jam, as he had taken so long on the creaming. He had to do all this therefore with everyone else watching, competitors and Judges too.

Competitors then left the room, were given a cup of tea each while the Judges worked out points. It seemed hours to Peter waiting for the verdict. The competitors crowded round Linda until all were recalled and judgment pronounced.

'You have won,' the senior Judge told Peter and then announced, much to Peter's relief, the reasons why. He couldn't help thinking that all the Rolls looked exactly like each other, so it was nice to hear that in consideration of texture, taste, lightness and some other finer points, his was the best.

After that came a triumphal lunch with Linda sitting proudly in the Winner's seat and holding Uncle's Certificate of Merit in her hand, together with an assortment of cookery books presented by McDougall's, the Gas Board and the Egg Marketing Board.

Afterwards he took Linda to Marks and Spencer's and bought her a new dress to celebrate.

'Now we'll go home and meet our public,' Peter said.

'And we'll put the certificate on the kitchen wall,' Linda said.

When all the children were at table for tea and Peter was hurling slices of bread on to their plates in the traditional manner, and after Grace had been said, Peter felt quite light-headed with happiness, joy even, at being the head and father of this mighty family.

'Children,' he said, 'from now on, no more rotten old bread. You may instead, as Marie Antoinette so rightly said, eat CAKE.'

16

Money Troubles

No wonder Peter sometimes felt exhausted. It was not cooking, cleaning, washing or being mother and father to 12 children that tired him. That seemed to him a perfectly normal day's work.

It was business worries that now made him sometimes silent in the evenings.

'Uncle, are you depressed? Can I help?' Linda said.

'Mmm, what's that Linda darling?' Peter said.

'Uncle's thoughts are miles away,' Pam said primly, 'you shouldn't interrupt him, Linda.'

Pam was the acknowledged beauty of the family and had a nice disposition too, though quite often her warmer feelings seemed to be lavished on her pet kittens and hamsters.

She was, however, like Linda in being acute at judging Peter's moods. Quite apart from the fact that, instead of giving the same attention to Children's Hour on television that they did, he often sat and scribbled figures on to an envelope or piece of paper.

The truth was that Peter had not—perhaps he never had—given up hope of buying more houses and starting more homes for children. Now that his family were settling down, he had plenty of time to think about it all, while they were at school each day.

Perhaps, too, though he did not admit it even to himself, he still dreamed dreams of the kind of life he wanted to give the children. He had wanted to 'rescue' as many as possible from institutional life. Now that he had his 'own' children, however, his ambitions were all the keener.

He didn't really like living in suburbia, even though the open country was almost at the end of the road. He had neither forgotten nor forgiven the people who, instead of sharing and wanting to promote his efforts, criticized and doubted his integrity. The terrible hurt done to him by cruel tongues still rankled.

True, it was different now. He had done everything he possibly could (he told himself) to show that it was never his intention to flout the 'law'.

He wanted this wonderful family of his to grow up strong and beautiful, living in free and beautiful surroundings— as in his own beloved, remembered Wales. He wanted to feel free. Yet he didn't FEEL free. Of course, it was wonderful having his best friend Anne next door, his mother and sister not far away. But Anne's presence and that of the others was also a painful reminder that once he had not been trusted.

Not that he let such thoughts up to the surface of his mind. They were there, nevertheless, unspoken, yes unthought:

He decided to try again!

He started to do business in Property Development which was something he understood. He would make money and use the money to buy more houses, rescue more children . . .

He went into the business of converting old houses into flats, starting in 1961 by buying a property for £15,000. Property Companies were mushrooming and doing big business everywhere, but he was confident he knew the market and could not fail, while the boom lasted.

He knew the owners of the old house. They were good friends of his family. They agreed to allow the development to take place before the date of purchase. It was only necessary to sign a contract to buy and do the conversion work, then to sell the whole thing and pay for it out of the proceeds.

Due to the kindness of these family friends and the way it was handled, Peter made a profit and they got their money. This roused him to further efforts.

He decided to do the same thing again, rather too ambitiously this time, before finishing the first job. Again it was a similar old house to be converted, but this time Peter was running a bit short of funds. Having got his own money tied up in the house, Peter then went to a bank and borrowed a loan by way of an overdraft; an action he was later to regret.

Then he made his fatal mistake. He decided to buy back the beautiful and elegant house, Kinnersley Manor, where he had started his Grand Plan two and a half years ago. He had sold it for £15,000 to a man who wanted to do the same thing, namely to divide it up into seven parts. So Peter went ahead and bought it back at the same price he'd paid for it. His Agent approved; the Architect approved. Then the whole scheme came unstuck.

The Bank started to hold back its funds until something was sold. They began to say they couldn't allow more development until the loan was all cleared; that is, he must pay what he already owed them first.

Peter owed the Bank £1,500 and the Bank suggested he clear the debt by selling Knighton Spinneys.

Peter was horrified.

'Do you realize I have got a whole family of kids here; we would all be out on the street.'

He went to Head Office to talk it over and managed to get time to put his affairs in order.

He was in a dilemma. Money had never mattered to him before, but now his own 'adopted' family were threatened.

Peter's mother had given Peter and his sister Pamela their share of her grandfather's estate. This Peter had long since spent on the children, on organizing and equipping first Kinnersley Manor and then Knighton Spinneys and The Brambles.

He would have to try and manage, as he'd never done before, living on the tiny residue he had left and feeding and clothing the children on the money provided by the Authority.

The question was . . . could it be done? With Christmas ahead?

Anne who lived with her family next door to Knighton Spinneys in The Brambles, was now too busy to help with the typing and paper-work, of which there was a great deal. Peter handled all the finance for both houses and gave Anne housekeeping money each week. So Peter had to do the typing and filing himself during the second year at Knighton Spinneys.

The bulk of correspondence was with the Children's Department of the LCC, and their Finance Department. There were times now when Peter found that by the end of the week he had no money left! Everything was proving far more expensive than expected. He had a permanent overdraft.

One trouble was that so often money from the Authority did not arrive in time. There might be some query on Peter's Demand Note which had to be investigated. Sometimes he had to wait more than three weeks while the Department checked and re-checked a detail in his Note.

'I wish', Peter said to Anne one day, 'that I could persuade the Authority that money must come second in a child's upbringing. If they can trust me to look after the children, they could surely trust me enough to send the money first and argue about mistakes afterwards.'

Meanwhile, little by little, excess of his spending over what he received, crept up each year. He spent each year about £500 more than he received and he was spending it out of the last of his own money.

The children were growing fast. They had to have new uniforms, shoes, raincoats, wellington boots. Knighton Spinneys overflowed with all their possessions.

Autumn had been expensive, with birthday parties for each child and a substantial present. Their weekly pocket-money money ranged from 2s 6d to 7s 6d at this time.

As Christmas approached, he sat alone in the evenings after all the children were asleep and all, except John, had been kissed good-night. He sat and worried how he would find the money to provide the family Christmas, which he believed they had a right to expect.

He told a woman friend who called to see them: 'I really don't know where our next penny is coming from.'

'I can lend you £200, Peter dear, if that will help.'

He accepted gratefully, promising to pay it back when some extra money arrived from the Authority.

He spoke of his problems. It had seemed such a good idea, to buy houses or land. Now, suddenly, there was a pile of bills for his house and Anne's and Patricia's. He'd bought a third house for Patricia and her five foster children.

'I had a bit of money of my own to start it all, or anyway something to offer as money,' he told her. 'I had a bit of property, enough to contribute towards the buying of Kinnersley in the beginning, to which the Bank added a sum by way of mortgage. Then on the sale of Kinnersley and the buying of the two houses, this one Knighton Spinneys and The Brambles for Anne, we were on the way. I thought I could juggle with my assets to the best advantage—.' So he'd gone on and bought a third house for Patricia. It was after that that he'd tried to buy back Kinnersley and gone into property dealings.

He told her, too, how he'd bought the furniture, some for cash and some by extended payments. He realized he'd spent too much on the contents in cash and now saw he should have gone more slowly.

'I didn't mean to be extravagant: after all it would be wrong to give the kids a completely false picture of everyday life. Yet, somehow, I may have done it, without meaning to do so. I've always been able to make money go further than most people. That was my mother's training partly.'

Later that day Peter sat with pencil and paper. He'd tried to keep the housekeeping sum stable at about £30 a week. He knew manufacturers' prices for all types of children's clothing . . . from a vest to a pair of socks. By buying at Marks & Spencer, he could save a large sum because school outfitters would charge much more.

He could keep grocery prices right down. No Baked Beans except at a special reduced price of 1s. He would buy tinned foods by the dozen when they were marked down as a special offer. No frozen food; that was too expensive but a 15 oz tin of processed peas for 8d or 9d was a good buy.

He could save by always buying mutton instead of lamb, and by buying only the cheaper kinds of steak and cooking it carefully, he could provide the children with meat as often as they liked. He planned the meals by setting the cost of the meal first and then buying the food to fit the sum. He chose a meal for its protein content. The evening meal must always contain 8s worth of protein, plus the bread and jam, butter, tea, milk etc. During the holidays, he fixed the protein value of a main meal at midday at one shilling a head.

It was essential for him to keep his knowledge of shops, manufacturers and their goods, up to date. He was prepared to cross the road six times in one morning to find a shop selling bananas at 1s a lb, apples at 1s 6d a lb and oranges at 6d each if they were Jaffas.

It was expensive, of course, feeding thirteen people but he was saving money all the time because of the things he'd done himself, right from the start, like making clothes, curtains and even furniture.

Somehow he would manage. But he must secure enough for his overhead expenses, i.e. rents, rates, mortgages, insurances, light, heat and repairs.

No wonder he felt exhausted.

Yet the whole enterprise in which he had become involved, to buy more houses and take more children, was a failure. In a mood of depression, he set about making Christmas puddings and cakes.

As he went about his preparations, putting up decorations, baking and shopping for presents, he brooded over his problem.

He must get away from this place . . . away from Horley . . . away from the Bank and their pursuing letters and calls. Away . . . but where?

17

Christmas

It was the practice of the County Council at that time to pay foster parents in arrears. This became a great hardship to Peter now, at a time when he was being pressed for money by the Bank. Almost all his own money had gone. Of course, he had been too lavish, he realized it now. He had spent too much money at the outset; after all, it was his own money he was spending and there was no reason to be careful. He loved to have an elegant house, not luxurious or over-furnished but to have a few good things. He saw this as all being a valuable part of the children's upbringing. They were to enjoy exactly what he had as a boy. However, the position now was that there simply was not enough left in his own private bank account to draw on for reserves. The Children's Money (as he called it) was always kept in a separate account, exclusively for their own use. After all, his was not a profit-making enterprise, undertaken for reward!

He put this in letters and messages to the Authority. He also pointed out that he now saw he had asked too little support money from them in the first place.

Back at County Hall, Peter's Demand Notes and letters were causing some anxiety to the Finance Department. Mr. Bolingbroke, Head of Finance for the Children's Department was not the kind of man often to be found in charge of the cash. He was kindly, generous even with the Authority's money; it was no part of his duties to refuse any reasonable request on behalf of the 9,000 children for whom he was statutorily responsible.

But now he was worried. One day he called his little 'Jeffcock Group' together into his office. They were at that time Denis Allen, Michael Fitzgerald and Monica Smith, the Child Care Officer. A rather select little group, naturally.

After all, the Jeffcock case was their responsibility and theirs alone.

Peter appreciated the sort of people they were, who put the children's interests always first. It was not for nothing that he had tried other County Councils and been turned down each time. In other words, they had not been 'big enough' in imagination and concept to risk making a precedent by fostering a family of children on to a single man.

They assembled in Bolingbroke's office to discuss what should be done. Fitz walked in leaning on his stick. Michael Fitzgerald had lost his legs in an accident early in life and walked on aluminium ones. He had enormous presence and influence on the younger staff who adored him. Denis Allen, who had recently exchanged his motor-scooter for a motorcar, took Fitz in his car when they went visiting.

Bolingbroke addressed them and read some of Peter's letters to the meeting.

'Aren't we going a bit over the top with this?' he said.

Costing the upkeep of children in care is a very elastic business for any Council. Natural fathers are asked to contribute, if at all possible, according to their income. The maximum demanded from a natural parent is £4 a week, but the average received is much lower and some parents cannot afford to contribute anything. Cost of keeping a child in a Council institution varied, however, between ten guineas and 17 guineas a week. For Peter, of course, it was nothing like this.

Nevertheless, the Authority were prepared to pay Peter more if only he would employ staff.

'I keep telling Jeffcock', Denis told the meeting, 'that if he will only employ staff, we can pay him much more than he is getting now. He knows that we would fully support him no matter how many staff he employs. But he won't do it.'

Fitz asked for the reason.

'Because', said Denis, 'he does not want anyone intervening between him and the children. He says that in what he calls a real family home, there is the constant relationship between parents and children and that's what he wants for them. It would solve so many problems if only he would employ staff; it would put an end to local gossip for one thing . . '

Monica Smith said that Jeffcock's children were beautifully cared for. 'I wish we had more Jeffcocks,' she added.

It was decided to ask Peter to attend a meeting at the Council Office for a full discussion. When he did so he explained his difficulties when he had to wait a month or more for the agreed maintenance money to be sent to him.

He said nothing about his troubles with the Bank, nothing about his recent excursions into property and high finance and his subsequent bitter disappointments.

It was agreed that in future he should be paid in advance instead of in arrears.

Afterwards Denis Allen did wonder if Peter had opened his heart completely about his financial troubles. He liked and admired Peter tremendously. He said to Fitz after that meeting: 'I like him. We did the right thing. But he is a reserved man; there will always be things he prefers not to say.'

Nevertheless, Peter wasn't going to let his money troubles spoil Christmas for the children. By mid-November Peter had put up most of the decorations, helped by John and sometimes by Willy and Terry too.

He cut holly from the garden, put tubs of plants in the hall and hung streamers and coloured lights everywhere. It took him weeks of shopping to build up the heap of presents until they covered the floor under the Christmas tree and made the sitting-room bright and exciting.

He hunted out the 12 stockings he'd kept from earlier years. He collected a whole bundle of presents from Granny and Pamela too.

Peter had forgotten nothing from those far-off happy Christmases with Grandma Firth at Retford. He filled each stocking in exactly the same order that his stocking had been filled then, 30 years ago. He put everything in as he remembered, placing a handful of nuts at the bottom of the stocking, then the apple, then the orange and banana, then the first toy, and so on, until at the top there was something sticking very obviously right out. This last sticking-out bit was intended to catch the eye; to show that between the children's last view of their stockings when they went to sleep, there, suddenly, in the morning light was a 'thing' sticking out at the top, and great bulges all the way down, which had certainly not been there the night before. It struck him that some of the older children were getting too old for this business. Then he remembered the homely Christmases they'd missed and went on preparing.

Next morning he was rewarded with early morning visits from Denise and Christine and Brian and Willy who climbed on to his bed to share the nuts and fruit.

'No, Dink,' said Peter to Denise, 'that's NOT the way to empty a stocking . . . turning it upside down like that and shaking it.'

Margaret came in, carrying the sweater he'd bought for her.

'Thank you, dearest Uncle darling,' said Margaret, seriously, 'I'm sure I don't deserve it.'

'You do, you do,' Peter said, with a rush of warm affection for his former ugly duckling. 'You deserve the best always.'

All rushed to kiss him. He tried to show them that the way to empty a Christmas stocking is to take the items out slowly, one by one, savouring the excitement of each and wondering what came next, until at last you found the nuts, and you could fling the stocking away.

He told them to get dressed and ready for Mass and he gave another parting kiss to Denise and pushed them all out of the room. He admired Denise most, of all the children, because of her courage. She had a bad arm which was not much use to her, yet she did more for herself than the other children. She never complained and just smiled at her own awkwardness. She ran out, holding her presents in her good arm. He looked forward to this day with his own fond family.

18

Whitsuntide

What happened next was all Pam's idea.

At Whitsuntide the family were round the table. They'd finished two legs of mutton together with the usual turkey, roast potatoes, peas, gravy and mashed, followed by the usual tinned fruit and Ideal milk 'pudding'.

The room was full of spring sunshine. Margaret had found some bluebells and put them in a jar on the table.

It was after meals that Peter liked to talk. He felt it was a good way of 'giving the children ideas'.

'How many of you know the names of the large towns in Wales? Can you find them on the map?'

It was his favourite subject.

John wore an anxious expression. He knew that if he spoke, he'd most likely get the answer wrong, and everyone would laugh. He screwed up his face as though thinking. Then he had a brainwave.

'Cardiff,' John said suddenly. He remembered he'd seen some big boats in a harbour. He'd tried painting a picture of it to please Uncle.

'Right!' said Peter, patting him on the back. He always felt, sometimes a bit guiltily, that if only he could give John sufficient time and explanation and self-confidence, he might end up the brightest of them all. In spite of many disappointments, he did persevere.

Paul just looked scornful. Babs had only one leg on the chair, and clearly, wanted to run and play in the garden.

Brian was playing with a toy gun, pretending to shoot Willy who was eager for a scrap.

Pam put back her thick gold plaits and said nothing. Suddenly Christine burst out in a sort of loud whisper:

'Aberystwyth.'

Everyone was silent with astonishment. Then there was a

loud burst of applause at her cleverness. It went on, however, just that few minutes too loud and long. Christine burst into tears.

Peter took her on his knee and kissed her. She snuggled against him, her blotched face completely hidden in golden hair.

'Tell us some more, Uncle, about Wales,' Terry said. Terry tried to say it in a Welsh accent and everyone laughed. Terry looked pleased. He was very much the actor and extrovert and was unhappy when not being noticed. He was the handsomest of the boys, dark and striking with a personality to match.

Peter launched into his favourite subject. 'I remember my childhood visits there so well. Especially one of the farms, Llwyndedwydd I think it was, where we were given bacon and eggs. I've never forgotten it', Peter said dreamily, forgetting that though photographed on his mind, THEY couldn't see it yet.

'Go on Uncle,' said Terry, 'tell what's it like . . . when you come home to Wales.' Terry sang the last words, to great applause.

Paul said: 'I expect Uncle's forgotten really, so he can't tell us.'

'Well, I did live there again before I had all of you, remember,' said Peter.

Suddenly Pam said: 'Uncle, let's go there.'

'How do you mean?' said Peter.

'I mean', said Pam, 'let's go to Wales for a holiday.'

'What ALL of us?' Peter said, 'how can we?'

'Oh Uncle, let's.'

It was the usual cry, but this time it persisted.

'Uncle, why not? We could go tomorrow.'

Well, why not? Why did he not think of it before?

'Well, not tomorrow, anyway,' Peter said, 'tomorrow is Bank Holiday Monday. And we never go anywhere on a Bank Holiday unless we cannot avoid it. But we could go on Tuesday.'

That settled it.

'What about booking rooms? It's too late for that,' Margaret said.

'Never mind,' said Pam, 'it's not important. We can always look for somewhere when we get there.'

That settled that, because Margaret never entered into any kind of argument with Pam. She simply became silent.

The room buzzed with plans. Peter felt excited at the prospect. So much enthusiasm. He would have the thrill of showing them his own beloved country.

Margaret went into the kitchen to make coffee for Uncle. There was a knock at the front door and Paul peeped through Uncle's nylon net curtains to see who it was.

It was the father of Pam and Christine with a woman Peter had not seen before. He came into the room in a gay, happy mood. Pam and Christine got up from the table and went to kiss him and the woman, apparently their step-mother. She behaved affectionately towards them.

'Pack your things Pam,' said her father, 'we're taking you both home.'

There was a stunned silence. The father explained they had at last acquired a house and now there was plenty of room for Pam and Christine as well as their other children.

Pam stood white-faced, unbelieving. Christine at first looked pleased and happy. Then she saw Pam's expression and she dropped her head so that the golden hair fell about her face, hiding it. She stood uncertainly, holding her father's hand.

Suddenly Pam regained her composure. 'We'd love to come with you Daddy, but we can't. You see we're all going to Wales on Tuesday and it's all arranged . . .' She plunged on, not looking at her father but looking hard at Christine, 'it's all booked and we're all looking forward to seeing Wales . . .'

Peter stood there, serious-faced, towering over the children. 'Pam I think you ought to go when your father asks you . . .'

H

There was an awkward pause. Some of the couple's ebullience faded.

'All right then, as long as you both come straight home to us when the holiday's over. If it's just a holiday, that's different.'

Peter asked the couple to stay and have tea and when it was ready, everyone sat down to eat and praised Margaret's cakes which she made specially because she was quicker than Peter; and also it gave Uncle a chance to talk to the visitors. Throughout the meal, Pam sat silent and stiff and pre-occupied. However, the cheerful, pleasant couple did not notice anything wrong.

'We'll bring Pam and Christine to you at Earlsfield on the way back,' Peter promised.

Later that night, Pam knocked on his door.

'Uncle, please can I speak to you?'

'Come in Pam, yes, sit down; we've had a shock, you and me.'

'Uncle, do I have to go?'

'Yes Pam, he is your father.'

'But Uncle, I can't leave you and the kids.'

Peter smiled; Pam was not quite twelve and she had a way of sometimes using important-sounding words. He recognized in her someone with his own liking for rules and order and a pattern to life.

Peter kissed Pam goodnight and said: 'You'll soon settle down there darling in your own home. And remember I'll always be here.'

Peter went to bed that night, shocked and as apprehensive as Pam was. How long would the other children be allowed to stay?

He looked forward to the journey next day, driving out with all of them round him, up the A5 to Wales.

Next morning Peter had first to decide how they would all fit into the van for the long ride.

He had earlier had to get rid of the Land Rover and buy the van in order to accommodate 13.

It was almost a mini-bus. A grey thing, still with its under-coat; which could have been a tradesmen's van bearing its own colours and titles painted on it at time of purchase. Peter and John had tried improving it with various bits of pretty enamel colours. It was ideal for the family as it allowed three children in front and anything up to a fairly tight-squashed ten in the back, if necessary.

Peter decided against having a real bus-type vehicle because this was associated in his mind with Institutions. He felt that a real bus of this type would be a horrid reminder for the kids of things which he, if not they, preferred to forget.

Also a bus had seats to it which restricted numbers some-what, quite apart from the low ceiling; whereas the van was high and comfortable. Peter, with his usual skill and flair, put an old sofa in the back and added two seats, upholstered, along the sides. The whole family could fit into the van comfortably plus luggage two or three feet high on a rack which he made from two car-racks. He got the local black-smith to shape it properly to cover over the whole of the roof. There were no windows except in the rear door so that once inside the kids were very privately enclosed in their own caravan. They could therefore sing all the way to Wales, and did.

Peter helped by John and Paul, packed the trunks on to the roof-rack. The pile rose at least 18 inches high and Peter covered it over with the fly-sheet from John's tent, roped it and boarded the van.

Next, arrangements had to be made for the animals. Pam ran here and there with her pets, handing them over to Auntie Anne and the older children at The Brambles with careful instructions. They promised to go into the garden of Knighton Spinneys every day and go round, feeding all the animals in their various houses.

'When shall you be back?' Anne said.

'Oh, sometime,' Peter said. 'We're not sure.'

He felt beautifully free, for the first time in several years. This was the life! Adventure, the open road, and the children. What more did he want? He smiled at Anne and waved goodbye to her and her children, who stood in a quiet, well-behaved group around her.

Well, no doubt there were two ways of bringing up children and who could say which was the better? Maybe his family did answer back. Maybe they didn't do as they were told. All the same Peter believed that children should be tough and individual and that was how he intended to bring them up.

With Margaret, Linda and Pam all helping, he soon had their picnic basket ready. He had some pounds of sausages left from his holiday stores, so he made pastry rolls and encased the sausage meat, and put it aside to cool. Next he sliced bread for the sandwiches, putting in six different fillings, including cheese, ham, egg, cream cheese, tomato and sardine. Then the bottles of lemonade and soft drinks were put in with some bottles of his own favourite wine, red and rough.

'Is this the kind you want, Uncle?' This was Margaret anxious to help as much as possible. She was conscious that the whole holiday plan had been Pam's idea. Nevertheless, Uncle would be sure to notice how helpful she had been. Why, if there'd only been time, she'd have baked some cakes.

He took the wine bottles from Margaret and packed them in.

'And your beautiful goblet, Uncle; will you take that as well? You know you enjoy the wine better . . .'

Peter looked at his beautiful modern and exquisitely-made copy of an old-style goblet in pewter. It was considered an honour for one or other of the children to be allowed to polish it.

'No, the goblet's too heavy and could easily get scratched', Peter said, 'instead we'll take my christening cup . . . I always take on journeys.'

He lifted the cup from the cupboard. It was silver and light and it was bent a bit anyway.

'Uncle's right,' said Paul, 'the cup's better. It's the right size so he doesn't fill it too many times before driving again.'

At last the picnic basket was stowed away safely. Peter had never felt so young and free.

He didn't even glance aside to see if any net curtains were being held aside to see their great caravan pass, as the whole family roared through Massetts Road . . . and on at last to the A5.

'Now kids,' Peter shouted to those at the back, 'remember my rule; NO drinks at all, absolutely forbidden for the first hundred miles. Then we won't have any problem.'

'Uhu,' said Paul, who always with his exquisite use of irony seemed years older than his $12\frac{1}{2}$ years, 'what sort of a holiday we're having, eh! No drinking, eh Uncle!'

'I do hope John won't be lonely and mopey,' Peter said.

John had to be left behind because he was back at work next day. John, now 15, had just got a job with a building firm. First of the family to earn a living!

'Now kids,' said Peter, 'next rule; all listen please. Terry, stop singing for a moment and listen.'

Terry was giving another full-throated rendering of 'we'll keep a welcome in the hillside etc.' He stopped when he saw that no one was listening any more.

'Listen,' Peter said, 'so I don't have to repeat it. Rule number one; we aren't going to stop anywhere, at all, for anything or for anyone, for 100 miles or three hours, which-ever comes first. Agreed?'

'Agreed,' roared 11 voices.

Peter went on to explain his rule. He always believed that if you only EXPLAINED to children, there would be no problems.

The journey to Llangollen was about 220 miles, mainly along the A5, in order to avoid the M1 which he considered too dangerous for his precious load. If they all kept to his timetable, they would have covered about half the journey before getting bored, too numb with sitting. And without that business of 'having to go to the lavatory'.

Next reason was that three hours was a reasonable time to elapse before they all got too hungry and thirsty.

He made their first stop near Oxford, on a pub lay-by next door to a Servite Priory which was a spot he knew well. Once he visited a friend, a dear friend just near here. The friend taught at the school attached to the Priory. He remembered that once—it seemed light years ago—he had gone there to discuss with a Priest friend of his, the Grand Plan. He had asked him what he thought of it. The plan was to bring up a large family of just such children as were at that moment sitting with him on the roadside outside, munching sausage rolls, sandwiches and swilling Pepsi and orange juice. He felt humble and grateful. It was suddenly a great pleasure to think back to those times. To think it had all come true!

There was, he knew it well, also a pub close by, a beautiful little place, centuries old and always so clean and sweet that he felt a secret admiration for the landlord. Quite apart from the equally clean and sweet WC provided for his customers. Peter proceeded to dispatch all 11 of them in turn, with many warnings.

'ALL litter to be carefully repacked and put back into the picnic basket,' Peter said. 'If we take advantage of this beautiful WC, then please let us all have the courtesy to behave with some decorum and treat it with respect.'

'What else, Uncle?' said Paul, opening wide, blue, innocent eyes.

'No cheek', Peter said, 'please, Paul; SOME people might expect such a family might become a bit scruffy and noisy, there being so many of us. I want no kids leaping from the back of the van. So hush now, no screaming, and put all the rubbish back into the van.'

Linda set to work to collect all the bits of paper and crumbs and the other children joined in.

'Now children, as a reminder, and in token of the service to which we are not really entitled unless we were customers of the pub and which you cannot be on account of your age, I shall go into the bar myself.'

'Make mine a Scotch please Uncle,' Terry quipped.

'I MIGHT buy some potato crisps,' Peter said.

'Do as Uncle says,' said Linda. 'Terry, Willy, bring me the empties.'

Peter went into the pub to buy something which he felt was due to the landlord for the use of his lavatory by 12 people. He wondered if the children were getting the message he was trying to teach them, about his ideas for gracious living. He fervently hoped so. Anyway they did seem a gay, happy lot which was something.

He suggested that, in thanksgiving for the journey, they should all pay a visit to the tiny little Priory Church belonging to the Order dedicated to Our Lady of Sorrows. It was beautifully cool and fresh inside. Peter made all the children say some short silent prayers for a few minutes.

He felt that, ideally, the prayers ought to have come before the various 'demands of nature' as he described it to the children, but consoled himself with the thought that God would not mind since God would understand that the calls of nature could not wait, whereas He could because that was the way He had arranged things.

Everyone piled back into the van. It was a Tuesday and therefore, according to the 'rules', the turn of Margaret and Denise to sit in front with Peter. His 'Dink' was so tiny, he said, it left plenty of elbow room for him.

The children sang all the way through Worcester and Shrewsbury and on into the threshold of the border country, where the Welsh mountains began to loom up above the gentler slopes of Shropshire.

Peter was deeply excited as they went over the bridge over the deep gorge at Chirk, with its notice by the side saying that here was the last pub in England (to remind Sunday travellers that there was a dry law in Wales).

It was such a thrill to point things out to the children. His home country.

'The English in me is now subdued,' he told them, then just to liven things up because the children were flagging a bit and were probably tired from sitting so long in a cramped space, he added:

'We're nearly home, kids, we're nearly safe from the enemy now, we've only to cross this long bridge . . . we fugitives from England are about to make the last mad dash across the drawbridge to safety . . .'

Terry became wildly excited. He started to sing . . . 'For he's a jolly good fellow.' All the children joined in, as the car raced over into Wales. Their voices were sweet and high and echoed along the valley.

'Look,' Peter shouted, over the singing, 'there it is, the word "Cymru". It means Wales. Pronounced Cumri. What about "Land of our Fathers" next?'

He drove through Chirk and along the fast run down into the valley where Llangollen seemed enclosed in its compact dimensions beside the River Dee.

'Hooray,' shouted Willy and Terry, though they could not really see much at the back of the van.

It was now late afternoon. Suddenly his own high spirits started to flag too. After all, he had 11 small children to find beds for before it got dark. What would they do, if they couldn't find any?

'Don't worry Uncle, we'll sleep in the van.'

At one house the lady said: 'How many did you say? We're not a school, you know.'

At another: 'You poor man' said the landlady, closing the door firmly. He heard her call through the house, 'Mfanwy, mind you lock the garden gate, girl.'

They found nothing in Llangollen and drove on to Wrexham and there was nothing there either, and returned to Llangollen just as evening was falling. The sun was sloping right across from one side to the other of the valley, with the young spring-leaved larches on the mountain just fading below the sunshine as it crept over the tops, while the opposite slope was shadowed from bracken-patch to boulder where, on that side, the top remained still sunlit.

They went back over the Dee, over its solid rock bridge, old and silent, and ran up into the town again.

Peter stopped the car outside a boarding-house four storeys high, where a Mrs. Roberts answered the door.

'Have you any rooms for tonight?' Peter asked.

Yes, she had. For one only?

'It's for myself and some children,' Peter said.

'How many of you?' she asked politely.

'For myself and 11 children,' Peter said.

'*How* many children did you say?'

Peter hesitated.

'Well . . . ' he said, 'won't you let me introduce you?'

There were stifled giggles from the van.

The lady peeped in at the front, but could not distinguish all the tangled bodies in the back. Besides it was already dark.

'Rescue is at hand, children,' said Peter hopefully

They began to clamber out, unsteadily, on to the pavement.

'One, two, three, four' the lady counted, quite cheerfully at first, as four neat, pretty little girls stepped sedately out of the van.

Then her face clouded. 'Five, six, seven, eight . . . oh my goodness me . . .'

But there were still Brian, Kevin and Terry to come. They clambered out, a bit sheepish now, shivering in the cool evening air.

The children stood in a ring round the lady.

'Is it a team then?' she said, with a backward glance at the van as though half-expecting the bats and balls to follow.

'No, they're all mine,' Peter said.

'Ah, and you left your wife at home for a good rest? I'm not surprised', said the lady.

'I'm not married,' Peter said.

'Oh.'

The children's tired feet shifting on the pavement, sounded out on the night air. Terry had a brainwave. Terry always did have brain-waves, no matter what. Where he led, the others usually followed, even Paul.

Turning his big, dark eyes upon the lady, Terry said:

'Please Miss, can I go inside your house for a minute?'

'An' me Miss' said Babs.

'An' me' . . . from Willy.

The lady knew when she was beaten.

'It's upstairs, first on the right' she said, and turning to Peter: 'Well fancy, Mr . . . will you come in and sign the book; a real handful for you, it is.'

Her eyes travelled over him.

One little boy looked up at her, grinning.

'We're a bulk order' said Brian.

Terry sidled up too.

'It was like counting sheep, wasn't it? Counting us?'

'Well,' the lady bridled, 'well, it's a bright little lad you are.'

But Mrs. Roberts had given up trying to make sense of the total chatter. She went into the house to prepare tea and beds. By nine o'clock, one hour later than usual, all the children were comfortably asleep.

They spent the holiday picnicking on the hills. Willy learned how to fish in the river and could not be dragged away—even at teatime.

That was the holiday that started it all. They had been into the 'promised land'. Nothing would ever be the same again.

On the way home, they stopped on the way through London to take Pam and Christine to their father's new house, as promised.

19

Flight

'Mr. Jeffcock, you might have warned us. Well, really, I give up. What will you think of next?'

It was Denis Allen on the telephone. He'd just heard from a Child Care Officer who'd heard from Peter on a recent visit to see him and the children at Knighton Spinneys . . .

Peter was going to live in Llangollen and was taking all the children with him.

'Oh no! Not just like that . . . without giving me time to prepare or anything. Really!'

'What a fuss,' Peter said, 'what's there to prepare?'

'Oh, oh' said Denis Allen.

Peter told him 'It's really a case of having found a beautiful house in the valley where we used to stay on holiday as children. My Welsh forbears had an estate in Denbighshire. We only sold the last part of it in 1946, much to my sorrow.'

Denis said 'Yes—well—maybe—but you haven't given me time.'

'What for?'

'To warn the Denbighshire Children's Department. They'll have a fit. I mean, they're not used to it.'

'Well, well,' Peter said, 'we are sorry to cause any upset. I honestly never thought it necessary . . . I've bought a house, a beautiful house. We're moving down there almost at once . . . yes for GOOD.'

He didn't mention that he'd paid £10,000 for the house, that is to say, he'd traded the mortgages on his two Horley houses for a new mortgage in Wales. Rather a clever move, in fact. Now the Bank couldn't touch him. Not that he was running away. They'd get every penny of the £7,000 he now owed.

The truth was he'd found a way of doing what he called 'juggling his assets' which would solve his money problems.

He'd persuaded the mortgagees to transfer the mortgage from the two houses in Horley to this *one* house in Wales. This left the two in Horley free of all charges. It was his belief that one should never give up a good mortgage. Not when it meant paying back mortgages at a time when he needed the money to secure the children's future.

Now by selling off all that remained of his own property, he could clear his debt with the Bank entirely within the next year or so.

Peter didn't know why he hadn't thought of it before. In the beauty and peace of Wales, he could forget all the troubles that had harassed him all these years. He would have the children safe. He could bring them up as normal, happy children without all this fuss. Officials arriving every month at least from the Department; asking questions, FUSSING . . . Away from Surrey, from suburbia to the peace of the mountains. It was going to make all the difference in the world to the children's health and development. They'd lose their Cockney pertness, their hot tempers. They'd become tall, strong countrymen with gentle manners and a love, like he had, for the Welsh valleys.

He was deeply sorry to have upset Denis Allen; or anyone at County Hall for that matter. They'd given him every-thing, his whole life; they'd given him the children. They were real friends, wonderful people.

It was only that everything had happened so suddenly. The children were wild with excitement, thrilled with his decision; they couldn't wait to go. They'd talked of little else since that wonderful holiday in Wales not so many weeks ago. Then, while it was all still fresh in their minds, John had got a holiday from the building firm. He wanted to see Llangollen too and Peter encouraged him. He'd gone on his bicycle—a birthday present from Peter—and cycled all the way from Horley to Llangollen. Peter was proud of him. John sent Peter a card; 'Dear Uncle, I'm sending you a photo of a fine house here. I think you ought to buy it. Love from John.'

Well, that was how he'd brought them up. That was what he wanted, expected even. He didn't want them trammelled as so many suburban people were by petty considerations of money or ambition. You took a sudden, great, adventurous decision.

The upshot was he went to see the house, fell in love with it and bought it. He was sure Denis Allen would be reconciled to the move, might even be relieved to get rid of this 'difficult' family; that he would remain their friend. Denis was so kind and good.

Another person also dear to him was even more upset. Anne Spence stared at him, bleakly, unbelievingly. After all that had happened; after all the difficulties, the problems, the gossip, the work, the sewing, washing, cleaning, cooking . . . No, it just was not possible. He was joking, of course?

'Why don't you come too? No, I don't mean to Ystrad Hall, though goodness knows, it's big enough. But we won't make the same mistake again of mixing two families in one house. But if you would like to come to Wales, I would look around and find a house for you and your family.'

Anne shook her head.

All she said was: 'I never thought you would desert me altogether.' There would be all sorts of problems now that she would have to handle herself, problems of budgeting, finance and shopping, taking decisions and, above all, being responsible direct to the Authority.

She didn't ask for all his reasons because she had a delicate sense of what a friendship permitted or denied. And he didn't tell her, except in general terms. In short, he was going, he said, because he loved Wales and it was a better life for the children.

If there were other reasons too, financial, personal, he kept them to himself. As Denis Allen had said to his colleagues: 'Peter always tells you only as much as he wants you to know and no more.' Perhaps Denis Allen, the Quaker boy brought up in a boarding school, did not quite accept that this sort of reticence was not necessarily a fault. It could also be quite simply the way that County people in Surrey, England, were brought up to behave. They kept their sorrows, like their joys, to themselves.

Ystrad* Hall was a beautiful, romantic house standing alone in the Vale of Llangollen, about a mile outside the town. The clean-ness of it! Peter felt he had truly come home at last.

It faced the River Dee at a point where the waters suddenly rose, leaped and eddied over flat, white rocks. It was an ideal spot for salmon-fishing.

Willy who loved fishing, was nearly beside himself with delight. But all the children seemed different now; they looked different, sounded different. Peter was convinced of it.

The move had gone smoothly. Of course, Harrods managed everything without any bother. It would never have occurred to Peter to shop elsewhere other than at Harrods; just as he'd in the past had Rolls Royce cars. They delivered the new furniture which Peter bought for the house on the very day they arrived. That was Lot 1 according to Peter's plan.

Lot 2 was the van from Surrey with all the old furniture and what Peter called 'our junk'.

Lot 3 was The Family, all eleven of them in the faithful grey van. Only Pam and Christine were missing—back with their father in London.

Peter had sold much of the furniture and carpets from Knighton Spinneys, as well as most of the beds and bunks. This time he bought an entirely new collection from Harrods, and this time they all matched.

He loaded the family luggage three feet high upon the rack; all the children got in and they set off. The Surrey van had already left. The proof of this was clear on arrival, for the men had emptied the family books, some three hundred of them, right on to the floor of the Conservatory. It kept them busy all that evening, just carrying them all into the house again.

* Ystrad—Welsh for 'flat land in a valley'.

As for Harrods, they were their usual impeccable selves. They unloaded the 22 beds ordered and took their departure in good order.

The 22 beds were to allow for holidays when Peter and the children hoped to act as hosts to other families and give them a holiday.

'Such grace and finesse,' Peter said to Margaret. 'You'd think, wouldn't you, they might bat an eyelid at 22 beds. They might say, "what's all this then?" or "expecting company?" Not Harrods, of course. I just had to tease the delivery men. "Had enough of beds?" They just smiled and said: "We thought it must be a school or something".'

'Oh Uncle,' said Margaret, 'what did you say to them?'

'I said, "No, not a school but we've got lots of relations".'

It wasn't exactly the Grand Plan with 100 houses and 800 children, but it was better than nothing.

Not that Peter gave the Grand Plan another thought these days. The extra beds simply helped to fill the great rooms. He was loving every minute of it. Peter was at his best at this sort of enterprise. Some people might have blanched a bit, sitting there among the remains of Harrods boxes, surrounded by junk and pictures and bits and pieces all over the hall.

Not Peter. He had carefully marked every piece with coloured tape and given the Surrey van a list of rooms for each colour. They'd actually got most of them right too.

He went to connect the electric cooker and sort out things for the evening, put up the television and so on.

Suddenly all the lights went out. It wasn't funny, Peter thought, in a strange house, cluttered with objects. How could he connect an electric cooker now when he didn't know his way around the house, let alone the dimensions of wall or floor or stairs so that he could at least creep up them?

The milk girl arrived at the back door having heard of the arrival and come to get their order. Peter rushed into the garden just as she was about to leave. He had 10 children in there, hiding in the darkness. The milk girl went back to the farm and returned with lanterns.

Shortly after that, a cheer went up from the children. The lights went on again, the cooker was connected, the television too. The beds were made, the food unpacked.

They finished off the meal in front of the television. They were truly home . . . to Wales.

20

Talking about Sex

After Peter and his family had been living at Ystrad Hall for almost a year, Pam and Christine arrived during the school holidays. Their own beds and all their possessions like books and toys and crayons and paints were waiting for them in their own drawers where Peter had carefully packed them away, so that no one else should touch them.

Peter was delighted to have them and there was a lot of hugging and kissing which went on so long that Linda said: 'Uncle, I'm jealous.' Pam and Christine had been given permission by their father to join the family in Wales for the holidays.

After unpacking, Pam said:

'Uncle, I want to speak to you. Important.'

'Yes darling,' Peter said, 'it's good to have you and Chris back. I've missed you terribly. We all have.'

'I'm never going back there,' Pam said. She was very excited, quite unlike his cool, lovely Pam.

'What do you mean?' Peter asked.

'Uncle, you've got to help me. To write a letter to my father. I want you to tell me what to say, and you must write too. Please, please Uncle. I want to stay with you and the others. This is my home with you; you know it is.'

Peter was worried at this. It was the sort of happening which the Authority always warned against. No involvement. No coming between the children and their real parent if they have one. What would Denis Allen say?

'But Pam, you can't do this to your father. It would hurt him too much.'

'I know but I can't help it. Please Uncle. I never will leave you again unless you send me away.'

She was weeping now and Pam rarely wept. What could he do? Then he said: 'What about Christine?'

He knew what Christine would do without his asking. She would do what Pam wanted, go where Pam was, always.

'All right,' said Peter, 'if you really want to stay. I'll write to your father and I'll have to go and see him as well.'

He knew he would dread making that visit. That night he wrote the letter to London. He said that Pam had decided that she wanted to live in the country and could not be happy in a town. They hoped that he would understand and Peter said he would come up to town in a few days to talk about it.

He tried asking Pam the reason for her decision. 'Oh yes, of course,' Pam said, 'they were very kind to us. Yes we got on well with our stepmother and the other children. Yes, it was very nice. But we didn't feel we belonged there. We belong here.'

Peter visited Pam and Christine's father and stepmother.

The father was bitter, angry and disappointed. He said to Peter: 'This is what comes of NOT sending them to a school or institution. They should have gone to a school like other children do and then this sort of thing would never have happened.'

Peter said how sorry he was and they parted, still friends but Peter was conscious of the man's deep hurt.

Then he returned to his family in Wales. He had all his 12 children with him once again, healthy and happier than ever before. He must remember to inform the Authority about what had happened with Pam and Christine and wondered, with no little anxiety, what they would say. It wasn't even legal to take children into one's own home unless they came from the Authority and with their permission. Well, he was not going to let it spoil the children's long holidays from school.

Now the long vacation had started, Peter decided it was time to give Babs and Pam what he called the 'low-down' on the Facts of Life.

He considered that at getting on for 12, these two were old enough. Babs had a large variety of friends in and out of school. Peter did not want the girls to go around without having sufficient knowledge. Or to find themselves in the position of not understanding what was meant by a certain word or phrase.

It was his opinion that ignorance was never a guardian of beauty and he was hopeful that the children would accept the facts of life as natural, see them as something with power and beauty. He didn't, in fact, want them to grow up to be either too curious or, on the other hand, too repelled.

His interview with Margaret much earlier, on these subjects, had been well received.

'I wouldn't want to ask a woman, Uncle!' Margaret said, 'she'd only tell me what happened to HER, and that might not be the same for me at all!'

Margaret at age 14, astonished him. She would never be as pretty as Pam or as gentle as Christine. Yet, already, there was hardly any trace left of the plain, resentful, argumentative little girl who had once caused him so much anxiety and depression. His ugly duckling was turning, before his very eyes, into a swan. She was going to be an attractive woman, that is, if only she would stop talking now and then . . .

To his surprise, she had wanted HIM to talk. It was she who raised the subject. He could hardly say he was an authority on the matter, but he felt it his duty to try.

'The difficulty,' he told Margaret, 'for women is that they are bound to see it subjectively, because it happens to THEM, and so you will get them saying this and that, and it might not suit you.'

'Yes, I see that. Well, I'd rather ask you, Uncle.' Margaret's creamy pale face and bright, hazel eyes were fixed trustingly on his face.

He thought what good companions he and Margaret had become. He could really talk to her now.

After this conversation, he found that he was consulted on

this subject whenever it arose. Now it gave him confidence to fulfil his duty as a parent and see that Babs and Pam were suitably informed. Not that he ever need, he felt, have a moment's anxiety about Pam; she was a composed child with a shrewd intelligence. Her flower-like face regarded the world coolly with an un-childlike assurance.

But Babs was beginning to change from a sweet though hot-tempered child into a sometimes wild schoolgirl. Babs was always the one who kept the bus waiting which picked the children up from school and brought them home. She liked staying in the playground after school to play with the boy gangs who came along for the customary chat-and-giggle encounters. It was unavoidable really, he thought. She was one of the most striking girls in the whole district with her red hair and freckles and violet eyes.

'Babs,' said Peter.

'Yes Uncle,' Babs said, looking up from her comic. Unlike Margaret who read books and novels, Babs had no intellectual pretensions of any kind. Babs with her sharp Cockney accent, her dislike of serious music or serious anything, was not just a philistine but proud to be one.

'I think,' said Peter slowly, 'that it's time I gave you and Pam a picture of the subject of growing-up and so on. You know, all about boys and girls, men and women etc.'

'Yes Uncle,' she said automatically, still engrossed in her comic.

It was 'late night' for Babs and Pam, so that everyone else was in bed when this conversation took place.

'Pam.'

'Yes Uncle.'

The girls were always polite. Some of his training had been successful.

'Come over here, both together. Then we can talk.'

They came; one sitting on the chair beside him, the other on the floor. He was delighted to see that Babs had even put away her comic.

They were accustomed to Uncle's 'talks' on general subjects. Both girls quickly became bored, however, if he
rambled, as he knew he sometimes did.

'Now, you know there are two kinds of people in the world
—men and women.' He stopped short. Well, perhaps that
was a bit obvious even for a starter.

'Yes, Uncle,' Babs said. Pam looked at the door. It was
going to be quite some time before she and Babs could safely
go through it and upstairs to bed.

'And you know I have always told you that I can't think
why girls like men,' Peter said, 'but they do, and that's that.
And if there were another lot to choose from, I am sure they
would choose them instead.'

Babs laughed. 'Yes Uncle, but there isn't another, so we've
got to lump it, you mean?'

'Exactly,' Peter said.

'Now Pam, what is the difference between boys and girls?'

Pam thought; her lovely face showed deep concentration.
She decided to play for time.

'The difference?'

'Yes. What would you think of as different about a boy,
for example?' Peter said.

'Oh that!' Pam clapped her hand over her mouth, laughing.

'Good!' Peter said with stern, mock-seriousness. 'I am glad
you notice there is a difference. At least, that's a start.

'Babs—you know where a baby comes from? Well, how
does it get there in the first place?'

'It grows in the Mummy's tummy,' said Babs, 'but I don't
know how it gets there!'

'Well, it doesn't start as a great big fat baby, now does it?'
Peter said. There was an imploring note in his voice.

'No, of course not,' said Babs, 'it grows from a tiny bit of
nothing.'

'Yes', said Peter desperately, 'but how does that tiny bit of
nothing get there? Is it there all the time?'

'It starts when the mummy and daddy get married,' Babs

said. Her expression said that she felt her explanation ought to be enough for any reasonable person.

'You mean,' Peter said, 'it is there all the time, and only when the mummy and daddy get married, it suddenly starts growing?'

'Something like that, I suppose,' said Babs.

Peter sighed.

'Right,' he said, 'let's start again. Pam, if the baby is there all the time and only needs mummy and daddy to get married, how is it that some people have babies when they are not married?'

Pam didn't look at him; she stared at Babs, nonplussed. 'I don't know,' said Pam.

The girls looked at each other solemnly.

'Uncle,' Babs began.

'Yes?'

'Pam and I are going to consult.'

'Right then' said Peter.

Their two silky heads went close together, Pam's gold on Babs' red head. They were giggling together he noted.

'Well?'

'Uncle' Babs said, . . .

'Yes?'

'We haven't a bloody clue,' said Babs.

He was rather pleased with the outcome. He felt it showed that it had been too early to broach the subject. Their innocence was untouched so far, he felt convinced.

'Time to turn the television up again? Then we can watch the film before bed.'

The interview was over. Not, however, forgotten.

21

A Shadow Falls

Peter and the children were enjoying a summer idyll in their remote mountain fastness. Peace at last! This was how life ought to be, he thought. If only everyone could enjoy this beauty and splendour, why there might be no pain, no more wars.

Back at County Hall in London meanwhile, for Denis Allen and others of the 'Jeffcock Group', things were something less than peaceful.

Once again Denis learned, Peter could expect trouble. Again people were talking and their words were nonetheless spiteful for all that this time they were in a lilting Welsh accent. What use would it have been to remind Peter that once before, he had been ill-used by mindless gossip? In the blissful peace of Llangollen, Peter thought at last he had found a haven where no evil could ever touch him again. However, he was wrong!

Some weeks before the removal of the family from Knighton Spinneys in Surrey to Ystrad Hall in Wales, Denis Allen had rushed down to Wrexham to try and 'sort things out' with Denbighshire County Council. As soon as he'd heard of Peter's intention to make the move, he knew that he would have to make the journey. There was a difference between London, the Metropolis, and Llangollen, a traditional and somewhat conservative Welsh town.

At first all had gone well. Denis talked it over with a charming and so understanding Children's Officer, Miss Leta Jones, Head of the Department. Denis explained the 'difficulties'. He outlined the history of the case and the sort of problems and difficulties already encountered. It was a worry for her, of course, he said. Problems might well arise again in the future, in which case he would gladly return to Denbigh to help, if he could, to solve them. They parted on the best of terms. Yes, yes, she quite understood and she was quite sure too; everything was going to be all right.

When next day Denis Allen returned to London, however, he was still worried. He knew that it was one thing to prepare 'the locals', but quite another to make them accept it— when it happened. He could only wait and hope.

Peter knew nothing of Denis Allen's visit. He was without a care in the world.

One day when the children were at school, one of the staff called unexpectedly. She said she was from the local Children's Department. She was in a very angry mood. She'd just been informed—by someone un-named—that a family of children were living in Ystrad Hall with a single man and no woman in the house. She was a new 'local' officer from Llangollen. Clearly, the Wrexham head office had overlooked the necessity of putting this lady 'in the picture' too. At least—not in sufficient detail.

The lady was not very polite, probably because she was so angry. 'We should have been warned about what was going on here,' she said. Peter did not ask her what authority she had to complain. He was so accustomed by now to this kind of hostility. She asked to see the house. Peter showed her over it with some pride. He felt when she saw the comfort and elegant beauty of Ystrad, she might calm down. But no!

'It is disgraceful that we were not told what to expect; what sort of thing was going on.' She said it was her duty to inform Miss Leta Jones, Head of the Children's Department in the district. 'I notice' said the lady in an icy voice 'that your bedroom has a communicating door to the girls' room.'

Peter froze. Then he politely asked her to leave.

Soon the telephone lines between Wrexham and London were busy with the story. Miss Jones was on the line to Mr. Denis Allen. And please would Mr. Allen come down to Llangollen at once and sort this thing out.

A little weary this time, Denis got out the car and drove straight down to Ystrad Hall to see Peter.

Moving the library. Willy gives a helping hand

Uncle with Christine and Linda, outside his
Surrey farmhouse   (*Derek Shuff*)

Opposite   The family grows up—some recent photos
1st row: John and Margaret *2nd row:* Babs and Pam
3rd row: Linda and Christine

Uncle—or is it Great-Uncle? A recent photo with one of the
next generation

It was about 9.15 am when Denis arrived and walked through the open front door and into the kitchen. He knew which way to go because he could hear the sound of music. He was struck with the beauty of the great house.

No wonder the front door was left open. Why, Peter had the whole valley to himself—except for the salmon in the River Dee!

Denis walked into the lovely old kitchen with its old wood chest against the wall, hung with pretty china.

At the sink, washing up to the requested tunes of Housewives Choice on the radio, there stood Peter doing his once-in-24-hours washing-up. He turned sharply; he was wearing a long green baize 'pinny' tied round the waist.

'Why—Mr. Allen—how are you?'

'Mr. Jeffcock, hallo . . . no, don't be alarmed. There's been a bit of bother.'

Peter said darkly that it was he who had had the 'bother'. He recounted what had happened with the lady visitor. He was in a sulky mood.

'But look,' Denis said, 'do try to understand; this isn't London; this is Wales; a small rural place and people talk. They've never had anything like this happen before in their whole lives.'

Denis told Peter that in order to stop the local gossip, he would have to employ a woman to do some of the work in the house.

'It's ridiculous,' Peter said; 'you can see for yourself. Wait till you see how happy the children are.'

Denis said: 'I know, I know.' He told Peter the lady had objected to Peter's 'communicating door' to the girls' bedrooms. He didn't want to upset him more than he need.

'Oh, oh' said Peter, 'these *dear* ladies love to complain and then they get it all wrong. It's the *boys'* room that adjoins mine—the previous owner's dressing room. What utter nonsense!'

Peter prepared a meal for Denis Allen and then showed him round the house. Denis was impressed.

'As far as I can see, you've done the right thing coming here, once we've reassured the people of the neighbourhood. This house is YOU. I have never seen anything so beautiful; and how tastefully you've furnished it.'

In the end, Denis enjoyed his visit. The children were delighted to see him when they returned from school. Denis thought he'd never seen them looking so well and happy.

Before leaving for London, Denis made Peter promise to find a woman who would come into the house, at least for a few hours a day.

Denis was given a room to himself for the night and left next day. It had been like a wonderful holiday, he told Peter. Peter smiled goodbye. He looked a little wan, Denis thought.

It was the first shadow to fall on Peter's dream home. A sudden mood of depression shook him. The first chill autumn winds blew from the hills through the gracious hall he had furnished so happily.

Here too . . . even here; would they never leave him alone in peace?

22

The Kitchen Mountain

A 'daily woman' was engaged. She arrived after the children left for school each day and left before they returned home again. Peter decided it was quite funny after all.

The Headmaster of St. Joseph's School at Wrexham was reported as saying, 'that family of children from Ystrad Hall at Llangollen are the best-dressed children in the school.'

Every morning Peter got the girls up first so that he could spend more time doing their hair. He liked them to look impeccable when they left home. They had a reputation to live up to now, or rather he had!

This summer he decided to make the girls' dresses himself. He was very fussy about the fit of their dresses and school uniforms.

'Come on Margaret, out of bed!' Peter pulled her curtains in the morning. No word from Margaret. She stayed curled up under the bedclothes.

'It's a lovely day,' Peter called through the blankets.

'Mmmm.'

'Get UP.'

'Give me a kiss,' said Margaret, still half under the blankets.

'Pest,' said Peter, kissing her, 'now wake up.'

He went out of the room and into Babs and Linda's room. One of the beauties of this elegant house was the number of rooms. There was space to breathe, to move.

'Beautiful day Babs. Want to see it?'

He rolled Babs from side to side in bed, without result. Then he went over to Linda and looked down at the brown hair spread on the pillow. His favourite! The whole family knew it. Well, he couldn't explain it. She was the only one really who never went against him, never got into a temper or called him names when she couldn't have her own way.

'Hello,' said Linda and stretched like a cat, then yawned.

What he enjoyed so much was the regularity of it all. The same words each morning, the same expressions or stretching movements, and the same reluctance to move. Children doing the same things at the same time each morning, how many thousand times? It gave life a pattern, for him anyway.

Next on to the boys' room. First there was little Kevin who was so small that he tended to get overlooked. Like his older sister Denise (Dink), Kevin was so tiny he could just as well have slept in a chest of drawers.

Kevin lay curled up, right under the clothes, silent, looking like a fused 'banger'. Peter touched the top of the tiny heap where the blankets crossed what were presumably his hip bones. And—flash—Kevin shot up and was wide awake at once. Like Denise, he was a pleasant, humorous little child and always sat cross-legged on the floor, looking like a Stan Laurel version of a baby Buddha. Kevin had the habit of eating anything left handy, even paper and rubber bands if they were nearer to him than food. He not only moved like a squirrel but he could shoot up a tree in much the same way.

Next to him in another bed lay Willy, always twisted as though in pain with his mouth open and a helpless, abandoned look he often had when he was awake. Willy was an unpredictable, mysterious boy. One day he would leap out of bed and on another he could not be moved before 11 o'clock.

Next on to Brian, one year older than Willy. Brian was the kind of boy beloved of lady novelists. He looked, even in bed, always the gay, cheeky, irrepressible but sturdy BOY. Everything about him, however, was neat and wholesome looking. He didn't lash about in bed like Willy; all bedclothes were still neatly tucked in as Peter had left them the night before.

'Brian!'

'Yes Uncle.' He was wide-awake immediately like an alert guard-dog, springing up at once.

'Terry,' Peter bawled at the next bed. The blankets were all pulled to one side, the sheets over the other and those bold-striped pyjamas covered a placid figure totally unconcerned, apparently, with this day or any other. Terry had his mouth open and he was quite happy to say, 'Good morning Uncle' as sweetly as he could, as long as he could keep his eyes closed and his body undisturbed.

'Sleep well. Call you again at dinner time,' Peter said, knowing that Terry would lie there for a while and consider whether this remark was to be taken seriously or not. Was it simply Uncle's day for joking? Or was there something special on today that he might be missing if he didn't get up immediately. Well, Terry decided, he'd just stay where he was and think it over.

Then to Paul, lying calm and alert by the window. If Peter tried any tricks with Paul, he would be sure to say: 'Saw you coming, Uncle!' If he really was fast asleep and had to be woken, he would then pretend that he had just dropped off again.

Paul never allowed anyone to think that he was ever at anyone's mercy by being in the throes of sleep. It was part of his acute defence mechanism which explained his apparent air of indifference and objectivity. He liked to pretend that he was always in command, always able to look after himself. Peter believed that Paul would have kept his socks under his pillow if he had reason to suspect someone else was short of them.

After that, Peter woke up the others or returned to the rooms just visited to give them a second waking which was usually necessary. Then he went downstairs where the breakfast table had been laid the night before. He let in the cat to give it breakfast, made a huge pot of tea, turned on the radio and made what he called 'morning noises'.

Other noises followed.

'How long are you going to be in there?'

'I want to go! I can't wait much longer.'

Or, 'Won't be long.'

A fearful crash came from the boys' bedroom; it sounded as though a bed had been turned right over.

'Morning, Uncle,' Margaret said, entering as though it was the first time they'd met that day.

Each of the girls went up to kiss Uncle before sitting down to breakfast.

Paul entered. No kiss from him. However, Paul was now 14 and too old for it.

'Paul's not the kissing type,' Margaret said.

'Some children don't like it,' Peter said. My sister and I both hated it. All those ladies . . . they used to call me 'kissable little chap' and hug me on their laps. Ugh!'

Linda loved to go 'adventuring'.

'Uncle,' said Linda, 'can we go up the Kitchen Mountain today? It was so named because this was the mountain right outside the kitchen window. Linda knew he preferred them to climb there because he could still see them in the far distance if he let them go on their own. They liked going alone, otherwise Peter would be first to reach the top which spoiled competition among themselves.

'I should think so. It looks as if it will be a nice day. Who's going with you?'

'Oh Kevin, Denise, Babs, Terry, Brian and Christine.'

'Yes, that should be all right,' Peter said, 'anyone else want to go? Willy, what are you doing?'

'Don't know. Nothing really. I'll stay here.'

He stacked the breakfast things and helped them with their arrangements for the outing.

The children took with them bottles of drink, orange juice or pepsi-cola and some impressive-looking sticks to help with the climb.

Margaret preferred to stay at home and 'help' Uncle. She was not an energetic person and liked nothing more than to sit outside and watch the river and its cascading waterfall.

However, heavy clouds soon began to gather on the Kitchen Mountain and Peter watched anxiously from the window. It was getting darker and the rain would catch them about half-way up the mountain. The telephone rang.

'Uncle, it's started to rain. Could you come and fetch us please,' said Babs. She had not got any further, in fact, than the bottom of the mountain. Babs, for all her wildness, had an alert prudence.

Linda, however, was way up the mountain with the two tiny children, Denise and Kevin. Brian was there too, all were soaked.

'All right,' Peter said, 'I'll come. Be there in a few minutes.'

When he found them, they were saturated, steaming, some with water streaming down their faces, and loving it. He had difficulty in persuading them to come down the mountain.

'We nearly got there, Uncle,' Linda said.

The children climbed Kitchen Mountain whenever they could, and the one further over, above Valle Crucis Abbey, where there was a telephone box. Peter warned that they had his permission to go up any mountain within sight of the house. But if they disappeared over the top and went down the other side (only allowed with special permission from Uncle), they had to telephone him and reverse the charges to tell him exactly where they had reached.

The result was that in that first year, Peter received the largest telephone bill he had ever received in his life, where whole columns were marked "Reversed Charge". It formed, however, a habit which the children were never afterwards to lose; even when abroad or when already working or when they had money jingling in their pockets!

So the habits of a life are begun. Far from diminishing Peter's pleasure, his was only increased. No wonder the children often said: 'We've got no money sense; nor has Uncle.'

At night, too, there were long telephone conversations

between Peter and Anne. They lasted about a quarter of an hour.

'We are all missing you,' Anne said.

The only one of the family who showed a proper 'money sense' was Brian who was known in the family either as 'the salesman' or 'the black marketeer'. Brian was always ready to sell the shoes off his feet if he could thereby make a profit. He often returned from school minus some item of clothing which, because Peter had bought it at a 'good' place or even made it himself, was sometimes of better quality than other school children had. He told Peter he'd found a 'customer' who valued it even more—in cash!

Brian was always making sorties out on to the mountain-side to look for items to add to the 'stock' he kept under his bed. Brian enjoyed 'the outside' more than any of the children, except Willy. Brian loved bird-watching and was often missing for hours doing it. 'Be warned, Uncle,' Paul said as he helped Uncle stack the tea things in the kitchen that night before the family sat down to watch television. 'Brian went scavenging as usual; he's got a shaped piece of clay he swears belonged to the monks who used to live around here hundreds of years ago.'

'It's a real find, Uncle,' said Brian, unloading his tray of cups and saucers on to the drain-board. 'I'm just having it dried out before showing it.'

'How much?' said Peter doubtfully. He was never quite sure whether to discourage Brian's obvious business or profiteering talents, or to encourage a possibly desirable and natural instinct for trading.

It was Paul who named his young brother the 'black marketeer'. And the name had stuck ever since Brian was caught red-handed by Pam in the garden of Knighton Spinneys one day, trying to sell one of her hamsters to some interested children.

Brian produced his 'find' from Kitchen Mountain.

Paul said: 'It looks like a chamber pot without any rim.'

Brian who always ignored any hostility or opposition, said it was genuine something-or-other and if Uncle wouldn't buy, he would offer it to the Headmaster or the History Master.

'That settles it,' said Peter, 'how much?'

'Make me an offer.' Brian grinned.

'One and six.'

'It's yours Uncle for two bob.'

Margaret shrieked. 'Don't Uncle, don't. Brian's got pots of money. He sold a stamp album to one boy this term, for five bob, and it only had two stamps in it. Brian told him they were rare ones.'

At least one of the children had a money sense. Which was something.

Peter was able to get on with a great deal of sewing on his sewing-machine once the family were comfortably settled into Ystrad Hall. At first he was fully occupied with making curtains for the new house. Some curtains he had brought from Knighton Spinneys, but this wonderful new home in the valley had 28 windows, so Peter set to work making new curtains and turning the hems like a professional.

It was after this that he decided to try, for the first time, to make summer dresses for three of the girls. He knew all the girls' measurements by heart, so much so that when shopping either at Marks and Spencer, or at local shops in the past, he never needed to refer to notes.

He was also skilled now at turning up a skirt, even pleated ones! He was the only really practised seamstress in the house, far better at it than any one of the six girls who were very happy to hand over all their sewing and mending to him—as well as their friends' sewing also! . . .

There was the evening when Babs brought a girl friend home to the house to have a bath. Peter didn't ask why she should want the bath in his house but said nothing as he could not think of any reason why she should not have a bath if she wanted to have one. She and Babs then disappeared upstairs.

'Uncle,' said Babs as she came into the sitting-room, 'Uncle darling, June wants to know if you would be very kind and take up her skirt while she is in the bath, and have it ready for her when she comes out.'

'Oh does she!' Peter said.

'Please Uncle, will you,' Babs said, 'June's skirt is a new one and it's much too long and she says she'll only make a mess of it herself.'

'All right,' said Peter, 'as long as she takes the skirt OFF. Tell her not to hurry her bath though or she may have nothing to wear!'

Babs knew that Uncle would be flattered at the suggestion that he could in fact take up a skirt in the time it took for a girl to have a bath. She also knew he would never think of refusing her anything she asked.

He remembered the last time when she'd just been about to leave the house and said: 'Oh Uncle, just stitch it please where it's come loose, or the whole lot will come down while I'm out.'

Uncle had turned Babs round only to find that the 'whole lot' was nearly down already.

'Babs, wouldn't it be easier if you took it off and I can have it done in a few minutes?'

'No Uncle, it's all right, I can stand still.'

Babs had stood; Uncle had turned her round to suit the sewing. In a jiffy, the job was done and Babs streaking through the door and out to meet her friends on the mountainside.

Peter finished the hem and was ready for Babs to come and collect it and carry it off upstairs.

The result was he decided to make their dresses in future. After all, he had cut, sewn, stitched and added several hundreds of yards of Rufflette Tape and made yards of pelmets for all the curtains. So dresses should be easy.

The reason was that in that year, St. Joseph's School arranged that material only, for school dresses, would be available at a local draper's shop. No finished dresses would be made in future, and parents were advised to 'make their own arrangements'.

'Don't worry Uncle,' said Babs, 'June knows a dressmaker who'll do ours.'

'I'm not competent, I suppose,' said Peter, 'is that what you think?'

'Oh no Uncle, of course NOT,' said Babs, 'I know you can do everything . . . June was ever so pleased with her skirt . . .'

'Why don't you leave Uncle in peace,' Linda said, 'don't you think he's got enough to do without you . . .?'

'But Linda darling,' Peter said, 'I have to be competent to make them whether I like it or not.'

'I don't see,' said Linda.

'And I don't see,' said Babs.

'Because,' Peter said patiently, 'how can I have my girls going to school in the summer term and being asked by someone where your dresses were made and you having to say "Oh yes, June's dressmaker made them". And then what, eh?'

'What?' said Linda and Babs.

'Then,' said Peter crushingly, 'what d'you think they'll answer? "Oh yes, of course, your Uncle could hardly be expected to do THAT, could he!" Yes, I know they'll mean it quite kindly, but . . .'

On his next shopping day in Wrexham, Peter bought an enormous length of dress material.

The pattern gave the dress a full skirt, gathered at the waist. It therefore needed, he felt, far more material than was required for his girls' 34″ or 36″ hips.

Peter laid it out on the dining-room table. He thought the lilac and white check gingham looked very pretty, only it looked like being enough for the whole of Linda's class, let alone his slender little Linda.

It was a huge dining-table for the 12 children, long enough for the material to be laid both ways across it. Peter walked all round it, trying to find courage to slice it here and there with his shears.

He opened the patterns and laid them out; there did seem an awful lot of pieces but he realized this was because the pattern allowed for two types of sleeve and he wanted the 'puff' variety.

He carefully lined up all the pieces, pinned them, checked that all were in the right directions, on the lines and on the folds.

He felt frightened at first to notice the gigantic length proposed for the skirt. He walked round the table again several times, contemplating the matter.

He re-read all the instructions on the pattern. Ah, this was an optional length! Even then, there did seem enough material for a ten-inch hem. He decided to ignore this problem and concentrate on getting the waist measurement right first.

He decided to cut out all three dresses in one go. It would be too tiring otherwise. Also, in the process of cutting up the first pieces, the 'dart' instructions would be cut off too, and he would be quite lost.

Better to cut the others while he still remembered where the darts were supposed to be.

Afterwards he bundled each dress together carefully, to ensure they didn't get mixed up, having decided to alter the pattern here and there, to suit each individual girl.

Linda was small with a neat shape and 34″ hips. Her waist, he decided, would look good in a gathered skirt.

Babs was rather more chubby and Margaret, then, even more so with 36″ hips, 25″ waist and arm and shoulder measurements vastly outstripping the others.

He swept the floor and went to get the evening meal.

Next day he took his sewing-machine into his study-and-junk room and set up a table on which he put his reels of Sylko, belt buckles, buckram and buttons.

Peter sat down, a bit depressed, in front of the machine

which bore the name 'Brother'. He thought of all the days he'd spent tied to it, making curtains for Knighton Spinneys and for The Brambles and for this house too.

The patterns lay around him as he started. Each one bore the bold lettering: 'Simplicity'.

'Oh Brother,' Peter muttered to himself as he began. He rather enjoyed the joke and even grinned to himself as he started his task.

Nevertheless, the dresses soon took shape. Except for putting the puff sleeves inside-out on the tacking stage, all went perfectly, though he found it tricky putting the band down the front, to take the button holes.

He did the button holes by hand which for him was easier, as he was skilled at embroidery, than doing them by machine. Anyway he had more confidence in his hands than in the machine.

Then the collars next and then the belts. They were straight pieces, sewn neatly over stiffening, turned neatly at one end over the buckle and stitched into a firm and even point at the other. After that he bored holes into them and secured them with eyelets.

'Margaret . . . Linda . . . Babs,' Peter called loudly over the blare of the television set, 'come and try your dresses on.'

He found he had to make adjustments to each dress to achieve a perfect fit and the hem on Linda's dress had to be done again. Then he sat down again for the final sewing.

'Come on Uncle, you've done enough sewing for one day,' said Margaret.

'I know what,' said Linda, 'if Uncle wants to sew, we'll make the tea ourselves . . .'

'There's my Linda,' Peter said.

'I'll make a big sponge cake,' said Margaret, 'please Uncle, can I . . .? You know you like my sponge.'

Babs said she'd promised to go for a walk with June.

At the start of the summer term, the three girls wore their lilac gingham dresses.

Peter made them parade in the kitchen. Really, they *did* look most attractive.

He admired the way the gathered waists 'fell' prettily. Linda said she adored hers because lilac was her favourite colour.

They wore the dresses throughout that term and they seemed to improve with laundering. The following season the girls were too big for the dresses. Peter put them away in a drawer and wrapped them, one on top of the other, in tissue paper. He kept the dresses for years afterwards.

23

Peter Confides in Margaret

Margaret, especially, was growing fast that summer. She had her 16th birthday party on the lawn. Instead of a birthday cake, she asked for ice-cream—10 lbs of it. She was thrilled about leaving school behind forever.

'Uncle, I'm *not* lazy. How can you say such a thing?'

'Easily,' said her Uncle.

'I got an 'O' level in History and three CSE passes. Was that lazy?'

'Yes,' said Peter, 'of course it was, you poor darling. Because it showed if you could do all that without a stroke of work . . . what could you have done if you HAD worked!'

'What about the prize I got for being the best girl in the school for that year?'

'Remember what went with it? It said you got the prize for being the "most-improved girl in the school." It showed what a horror you were the year before.'

'Oh Uncle, you are . . .'

'Are what, dear?' Peter said, putting his hands on her waist where she was uncontrollably ticklish, 'are what?? Careful now, or I'll tickle you!'

'You are . . . lovely!'

She backed away, laughing. Peter followed.

'Babs, Babs!' Margaret shrieked . . . her voice echoed throughout the house. 'Babs, come quickly.'

Babs came. 'What?'

'Let's tickle Uncle,' Margaret said.

Linda soon joined in. The result was that Uncle was laid upon the floor, struggling and protesting with mock feebleness. They had felt his strong hand on their bottoms from time to time and knew perfectly well, as he did, that he could dispose of three of them with one hand tied behind his back, if he wanted.

They were the happiest days that he always liked afterwards to recall. He used to say: 'Do you remember, Margaret, when I locked you all in until you begged for mercy and made a solemn promise never to tickle me again, if I let you out?'

Margaret, the child he once thought he could never love, was now very dear to him. She was his eldest; and he felt it natural that he should confide in her his new worries.

He took her one day for a shopping outing in Llangollen. Before going home, they went as usual to the Church. Peter always parked the car there, before or after shopping, so that they could go in for a few minutes.

When they came out again, instead of driving off, he sat there. He must talk to someone.

'You know, Maggie . . . things are not right for us here . . . there's something wrong somewhere . . .'

'How do you mean, Uncle?'

'Well, every day now, I get the impression that we ought to be back in Surrey. It worries me so much, I feel I can't stand the strain any longer.'

For Peter, with his reserve and reticence, this was quite a speech. He could say 'I am worried', or 'I am happy'. To describe either feeling in detail was something quite beyond him.

Peter did not tell her what lay behind the worry.

What worried him were the angry letters he'd received from several of the children's real fathers. These protested to him, as well as to the Authority, that Peter had never had any right to take the children so far away.

It made Peter feel bitter and hopeless to read the letters. How often did the children's fathers ever contact the children anyway? Surely, what mattered was that here in Wales, Peter had been able to give them the Good Life.

'Oh Uncle,' said Margaret, 'do we HAVE to leave this beautiful place? All us children love it so. Oh Uncle.'

Peter sat there, staring out at the glorious hills. Each day the sun came up over the top, wound its way round the valley and shimmered on the far side, through the dark evergreens covering the side of the mountain. How he loved the old river, centuries old, yet still narrow and slow except when the rains came rushing over rocks and boulders to make that private swimming place at the very bottom of their own garden, below the steep bank where rhododendrons grew as thick as daffodils. He loved the thin mist that rose on winter mornings and drifted through the bedroom windows as the day began, just before the sun came to warm the valley. He loved the thin streaks of grey smoke which rose from each cottage, high into the pure air and vanished into the light.

'I know, Maggie dear, I just can't bear the thought of our leaving and I haven't the courage even to mention it to the other children. But I can talk to you . . .'

'Yes, dearest Uncle darling,' said Margaret. 'But you don't tell me why! Why must we leave here?'

He did not answer. Besides, what really was there to tell? A few letters—a few words from Anne on the telephone. A hint—a word—no more. But it was enough to make him feel guilty!

After all, he'd started it all, it was a big responsibility for Anne, for Patricia, trying to cope with angry parents perhaps? Did they all envy him his 'paradise'?

He said 'I wanted us all to stay in this house until everyone was grown up . . . stay forever if you felt like it . . . just like a real family. After all, in a real family, not everyone wants to go away or get married. This house was my idea of something utterly desirable. High ceilings, space. I get so depressed in cramped, small rooms with low ceilings . . . do you remember some of the houses in London and Surrey, Maggie dear? Did I tell you when I was a boy . . . I grew and grew like Alice, I always hit my head on the oak beam across my bedroom ceiling . . . '

'Oh Uncle, can't we stay, can't we . . . ?'

'You don't know, Margaret darling, what it's like. Auntie

Anne isn't the only one . . . not by any means . . . every-one reproaches me. Every telephone call . . . every letter. Everyone tries to make me feel I did wrong to bring you to this beautiful place . . . so far from where you belong.'

'We belong here now, Uncle. You said yourself you never knew that Willy and Terry could be so little trouble to you. They're never naughty and rude like they used to be. Willy told me he just wants to sit by the river fishing forever and never move . . .'

Margaret put her arm round his shoulders, lifted her face to his and kissed him. 'Uncle, if you think we must, then I suppose there's nothing else for it.'

'You see darling,' Peter said, 'there have been so many difficulties . . . family troubles. I won't go into it all now. Denis Allen said when we first came that he was a bit worried about our coming here, so far from London. Then there was the lady who called here last year and tried to stir up trouble. There are other people too who say you girls shouldn't be so far away, unprotected, out in the country, isolated with me.' He laughed bitterly. 'For a long time I tried not to think about it. But it's gone on and on . . . I never really feel free. Always the same, hints and reproaches . . .'

Peter was grateful to Margaret for letting him talk to her like a grown-up. Then she suggested that even if they did return to the south, it need only be for a year or so.

'Let's keep the house, Uncle, let's never part with it and then we can come back again.'

This seemed a good solution, Peter thought. The whole family could come back and spend every holiday at Ystrad Hall. They need never really leave it for long. He could rent a temporary house for the family in Surrey. This would always remain their real home.

They went home that day and Peter felt more at ease now that he had come to a decision.

Next day he took the children with him to explore the

valley again. He drove straight up the road leading to the top of the nearest mountain, right through the sloping woods of the Forestry Commission until they found a stream.

The children built a huge dam and for several hours they splashed and paddled in the water until it was time to start hurling stones and rocks in competition, to break the dam to pieces again. Then Willy fell completely in the water.

Peter who was an excellent swimmer, had taught all the children to swim. The others shrieked with laughter at the sight of Willy, shedding water on the bank.

'And me . . . and me,' shouted Terry and was about to plunge in.

'That's enough,' Peter said and hauled him back with one hand while he held on to little Kevin with the other. 'If we go on like this, throwing stones, the water will start to boil.'

Back in the estate car he'd bought after giving up the van, he made the children dry off with the towels he'd bought. Then he stripped Willy, rubbed him all over with the rough towel, and dressed him in new sweater and shorts.

It was too early to eat so they went through the valley to the old Abbey of Valle Crucis, standing between a farm and a caravan site. Half the roof had been roughly mended by the Ministry of Works with sheets of corrugated iron. He made the children walk with him through the ruins and smooth grass while he told them of the Catholic past of the Abbey. He never tired of trying to interest the children in the things that interested him.

'This is where Mass was celebrated,' Peter said, 'monks used to work here in these fields. Sometimes terrible things happened here . . .'

Linda said: 'Uncle, why did people want to become monks?'

'People wanted to take a step towards God', Peter said, 'to seek His wishes, ask forgiveness for mistakes, in all simplicity as children do.'

He studied the children's faces, crowding round him. Impossible to read their expressions. However, they did not, he thought, look bored so he hoped they didn't feel he was 'forcing' them.

'Look, Paul,' Peter said, 'the pillars on the eastern facade; they've stood straighter than any Guardsman, three hundred years without even being looked after. No roof to protect them from erosion, no stonemasons to keep birds and bees away.'

'Mm,' said Paul, looking up at the pillars. 'Very pretty.'

Peter said it was nearly time to eat, but first he would like them to stand under the pillars and recite the Rosary.

Later they climbed the mountain and wandered, looking for a spot to light a fire and cook the food brought in the van with them. Peter found a sheltered cutting beside the road and unloaded the iron grid from the van.

The children were told to collect rocks and then Peter laid the grid across them and lit a fire.

'Collect as much brushwood as you can,' Peter called to the children, 'you'll find it scattered all over the place.'

Denise, as usual, was back with the most. Then Brian raced up, puffing hard. Brian was the only one of the children to show any promise in athletics. He could run faster than anyone at school and Peter sometimes ran with him, to help him train.

Peter put the enormous Aga oven pan which his mother ('Granny' the children called her) had loaned to him and put the lard into the pan. The fire was really hot. The fat was at its best, fierce but fanned by a light breeze so that it was less of a danger than when the children crowded round the stove at home, pushing each other to get closer.

'Everyone sit round,' Peter said, 'have your plates and knives and forks ready.'

He served each child with bacon and eggs, while Margaret and Babs handed round slices of bread.

'Yum yum, delicious,' Paul said.

'Uncle, can we have another picnic tomorrow?' Babs said.

A crowd of youths and girls were seen climbing laboriously

up the mountain far below. It would be a long time before they came level with the picnic.

Peter boiled water, carried in a five-gallon drum, and made a mug of tea. As he put the water on to boil again for the washing-up, the party of young people came into sight.

Margaret said: 'Oh Uncle, when I see other people, I feel so sorry for them.'

Everyone was helping to tidy up and pack things back into the estate car again.

'Don't you want to know why, Uncle dearest darling,' Margaret said, 'I mean why I'm sorry for other people?'

Peter smiled at her.

'Because they aren't us. Because they can never be as happy as us, in our happy family life. Oh Uncle, aren't we lucky, all us kids?'

Peter knew, he felt, who was the really lucky one this day.

He decided to put off telling the children that, after only two years, he was going to move them again. He would wait until . . . well, he would wait.

24

Peter Breaks the News

He had been thinking of nothing else for days. He rehearsed
what he would say to the children.

When they were all seated at lunch round the table, Peter
announced that he had something to say to them. He added
that it was something rather 'difficult'.

No one said anything. The children knew quite well that
whatever it was, it was going to be something unpleasant.
They knew Peter's moods exactly and could always sense
when something was wrong.

Peter looked at their fresh, healthy faces all turned
towards him. He felt he loved each one, as never before.
They belonged to him. They did belong, he felt, in spite of
all the studied hints, the reproaches that reached him.
He was bound to them now, and they to him. His family.

'I have some sad news to tell you,' he said. There was a
total silence. He forced himself to go on and say the hated
words.

'We will have to go down to Surrey again,' he said.

The storm burst. 'Oh no!' said Willy and looked as though
he was going to cry. Willy stood up suddenly, pushing back
his chair and raced from the room.

'No, leave him alone, Linda darling,' Peter said, 'I hate
telling you all this news just as much as you hate hearing it.
But we are in a difficult position.'

'But why, Uncle,' asked Paul.

'Oh Uncle,' said Denise and Brian and Kevin.

'Must we?' said Babs, always the realist.

'Is it because of old . . . ?' Terry began and then stopped.

'Do we have to?' said Linda. There were tears on her
face.

Babs said: 'I can't even cry. I feel I'm crying inside.'

Linda got up and put her arms round him. 'Don't worry Uncle,' she said, 'please don't be unhappy.'

Paul tried a feeble attempt at a joke. 'Ah well, that Headmaster'll be glad I expect.'

Headmaster of St. Joseph's, Mr. Cleary, was a special favourite of the whole family. It was Paul's wry way of saying how much they liked him.

Peter had already decided never to reveal that one of the children's fathers had written to him an unpleasant letter, and sent another to the 'Authority'.

Peter was saying something about 'You see, I couldn't take the strain of it all any longer.' The faces round the table stared back—waiting. 'I got letters—calls' he said, 'from London. It caused me constant anxiety.' He stopped abruptly. 'So you see—we must go back.'

The room emptied silently. For a long time, Peter sat there staring. He heard a sob from behind him. It was Christine, tears running down her face; she wanted to be comforted.

As he sat there with Christine on his knee, stroking her long gold hair, Brian came back into the room.

'Not to worry, Uncle,' he said, 'you know those new beds you bought us from Harrods. I know someone who'll do a swap for them; it's a friend of mine in the village; he'll give you a good price for them, Uncle.'

When the family re-assembled for tea, Peter said, in an effort to cheer them, that he intended to ask the Headmaster to keep their places in school.

He explained his plan. They would have to go 'down' for a year or so, but they would all be coming back. He would not sell the house but only let it, just as it was. There was no need for anything to be changed. Mrs. Ellis who 'came in' for a few hours each day would be asked to live in the house as caretaker.

'You'll see', Peter said, 'it will only be temporary. We shall be back the very first minute; the first holiday.'

They seemed slightly cheered, but listless. The tea things were stacked away and the television switched on.

Next day was a Tuesday, the day of the week when he did the weekly wash. Wednesdays he did the ironing.

He counted the garments as he put them into the washing-machine; there were 12 school blouses and 26 shirts.

Christine came rushing in after school. 'It's John,' she said, 'he's come back.'

John had for some months been working as a porter in a local hotel and doing well. He told Peter earlier that he planned to ask for a rise in pay.

John stood there in the kitchen, as Peter straightened up from the washing-machine, wiping his damp hands on his apron.

'Hallo John, I didn't expect you, on a Tuesday afternoon. Got a day off?'

'I've been fired,' John said, 'he wouldn't give me the money.'

Peter said: 'Never mind John, we'll talk about it later. We'll think of something else for you.'

Well, that was going to be another worry. John didn't always get on well with people. He was a charming boy, Peter thought, but he wasn't quick in understanding.

Peter was thinking of his plans for the family's return to the south. It was time for Margaret to get a job too. They would have to discuss what she would like to do. Soon it would be the turn of Terry and Babs and Paul . . .

His family were growing up. He couldn't help feeling they had all started really to grow up the day he announced they would have to leave Wales and go somewhere else.

Peter decided to drive down to Surrey and start looking for a house. He took Margaret with him, in the new red sports car he'd just bought, and Mrs. Ellis moved into Ystrad Hall for the few days he would be away.

PART THREE

Peter Grows Up with the Children

25

Suburbia Again

Peter found a house with four bedrooms, fully furnished, back in Horley, Surrey. He could rent it for two years.

He returned to Wales to tell the children who accepted the news without enthusiasm.

At last the move was finished. When they reached their new home, it looked quite cheerful. Anne had been there earlier in the day; she'd turned on the central heating, put flowers in the sitting-room and Welcome Home cards on the mantelpiece.

The children went to bed in a strangely quiet mood. It had been rather like coming on holiday to a disappointing place; after all their best possessions and belongings had been left behind, up 'there' in their real home.

Mrs. Ellis had given a solemn promise to leave everything just as it was. Next spring they would be home again and everything would be just as it was before.

Ah, but he must not, Peter told himself, get so depressed. He never felt like this before.

If only the semi-detached suburban house in Surrey were not such a contrast with the romantic mansion they'd left behind.

Anne, of course, was glad to have him back. They compared notes, sitting in her shining, orderly room with the bay window overlooking the tree-lined road. The curtains he had made for the house were in the windows; all was in good order.

'You know, Peter, I think I have done pretty well. I have nine children and never had a husband. What do you think of that, eh?' She laughed.

'If it comes to that', Peter said, 'I have twelve children too but no wife. Isn't that even more remarkable?'

They talked about the children. Did Anne think they were settling down again after all the upheaval, Peter asked her.

'Yes and no,' said Anne.

She found some of the boys were changed. 'Terry, for instance, he likes to fight with my boys. I don't allow it.'

Yes, she knew that Terry always liked running to her house. He was fond of her, she knew it. Yes, she felt she could always calm him down.

'Willy,' said Peter, 'what about Willy?'

He'd come home from school with a damaged face the day before.

'I get worried about Willy', Peter said, 'I really feel that leaving Wales was a great shock to him. He loved it almost too much up there.'

Anne did not tell him what she had learned from Terry. Willy got into fights at school because the boys said 'rude' things to him about Uncle. They jeered at Willy, saying his uncle was 'queer'.

It was from Babs that he later heard the news. Then from Willy himself.

'I hate this school,' Willy said. 'I hate this place. I wish we'd never left Wales.'

Peter asked him what had happened at school.

Willy told him the children teased him. 'Tell us,' they kept saying after school, in the playground, 'what goes on in that funny house.'

Another boy came up and said: 'And tell about that queer man you live with.'

'And so?' Peter said.

'I just hit him,' Willy said.

That was the evening Willy came home with a bruise on his face. Instead of watching television with the other children, he said he was going out for a walk. He returned and went straight upstairs to bed without saying good-night to anyone.

Peter felt depressed that night. John was in the Army, serving with the Royal Welch Fusiliers in Wales, Margaret was spending the night with a friend in London. The father of Linda, Denise and Kevin had written to say that he wanted his children back.

Was the family really going, leaving him . . . so soon?

26

Babs

The house in Wales seemed very quiet when they returned for the long summer holiday as he'd promised. The family was so small without Babs, Paul and Margaret that Peter found he hadn't enough to do and he started painting again. But it wasn't the same, he found, without Margaret. Margaret used to make coffee and bring it out to him as he sat, facing the river with his easel, brush and paints. Margaret's voice was like a river; it flowed on and on sweetly. He was accustomed to it and missed it.

To the hostel in London where she was staying with a girl-friend (both girls were planning to learn shorthand and typing), Peter sent letters to Margaret.

'Hello old Darling,' he wrote to Margaret, 'I don't really know how I should get used to being without you altogether. It's very odd—I keep expecting you to walk in, or be making coffee, or just chattering. It's certainly quiet without you (in the nicest sense!). And every time I look in the shops, I say to myself: 'Would that be nice for the old Darling?!' Have a good holiday—God bless—Lots of Love, Uncle Peter.'

His second letter said: 'If you can't come home with Granny I promise, DV, to come and fetch you myself and so don't worry any more about that—I enclose some more money to spend just for pleasure. God bless and much love from "A Different Uncle" since you went away!'

His third said: '*Very* quiet here now—much too quiet, I suppose, but certainly much easier to hear oneself speak! Enjoy yourself—go and see Granny and everyone else you know and come home again as nice as ever. Just getting Sunday dinner, Love to all and a big hug for you—Uncle.'

He missed each one of the children when they were away from him. Only this time, it really *was* quiet. Babs and Paul had both been left behind in Surrey, now they had started work. Paul had a labouring job for some building contractors and Babs was doing unskilled work in a small local factory. Their very first jobs!

He did have more time for John who was at home again on leave, having joined the Army that year. John was busy all day doing woodcarving or making shelves or cupboards. John also had a very considerable talent for drawing.

Still the unusual quiet got on his nerves. He preferred it when all the family were together. But the house was as beautiful as ever, and everyone happy to be back there.

The telephone sounded out sharply above the murmur of the river. It was Anne. She was worried about complaints she'd heard from the neighbours. The complaints were from people living near the semi-detached house which Peter had rented on the return from Wales. They said that their sleep was being disturbed by 'wild parties' in the house.

Well why not, Peter thought. He always encouraged all the children to bring their friends home. It was better than having them go out and stay out late, especially if he didn't know where they were or who the friends were. Certainly, it had proved expensive and even tiring sometimes, having to make coffee and cut sandwiches all evening for whole crowds of friends, but he preferred it. He really did. He preferred it anyway to worry and anxiety.

Anne said on the 'phone she had not been able to visit the house (how could she with a large family of small children of her own to care for?) but she'd heard talk, probably just gossip, about 'wild teenage gangs' coming and going into the house.

It made a gloomy end to the holiday. Peter packed up, said goodbye to Mrs. Ellis, handed over the keys and instructions for his next visit and drove the children back to Surrey.

The house was in a mess.

Babs said: 'I'm awfully sorry Uncle. I did invite a few

friends, but a lot more turned up than we expected. They kept on coming.'

Peter toured the house. Babs had done her best with soap and hot water to remove the remains of her 'entertaining'. The worst damage was from cigarette burns on tables and chairs and furniture.

The kitchen was chaos. Many of his willow pattern cups and saucers lying smashed with shattered glasses, dirty sausage ends, half-eaten pies. Several windows were broken. Babs, silent now, worked away trying to restore order.

Nearly every room in the house seemed in chaos.

'Some of them started a game,' said Babs, 'it got out of control.'

Peter said nothing. What could he say? She had told him that she had tried to restrain her friends; she had said it was not her fault. He had made it a rule always to accept what the children told him. After all, Babs was only 15.

He said to Paul: 'Tell me what happened.'

Paul said: 'Look Uncle, it's nothing to do with me. Babs invited all these people. None of them were my friends. I just kept out of the way.'

This remark seemed to sum up Paul's whole attitude to life. 'You never like to be involved, do you Paul?' said Peter. Paul shrugged and left the room.

Peter set to work to try and remove traces of any damage to the house. Later the owners of the house sued for compensation for the cigarette burns and other repairs. They asked £800. In the end Peter paid £300 in order to settle the matter amicably.

Now that he had paid off the £7,000 he owed to the Bank, he could think of looking around Horley for another house to buy.

Meanwhile he informed the Authority that he needed more money to run the household and it was agreed that he should get a 'rise'.

Soon afterwards Peter took a 5-year lease on an attractive

homely part-16th century house called Lovelocks Farm at Horley at a rent of £800 a year.

Now the incident of 'poor old' Babs' parties in the former house could, he thought, be properly forgotten.

The trouble was, though, that Babs at 15 years of age, was quite a different person.

She was so changed, it was hard for Peter to recognize the 'nice little girl' who had come to him five years ago, to be in his First Family.

He moved them all into Lovelocks and everyone was happy about it. The house stood in twenty acres of fields. Pam moved her pets into a charming room of her own, overlooking the fields. Peter unpacked his painting canvases to finish those he had started to do while in Wales.

'Don't you think I'm right?' Peter said, 'that 10.30 pm is late enough for any girl of 15?'

'Oh I do,' said Anne, 'My girls are never out so late.'

Peter explained that Babs was getting quite beyond his control.

'She wants to go out 365 nights in the year,' said Peter. 'If I try and stop her, she fights me like a wild cat. Or a tiger even. I tell her she's got to stop in at least one night sometimes to do her washing or make her bed. She sulks while I'm talking to her.' He sighed. 'Your children are so different.'

Anne said: 'I am stricter than you are, certainly. I've always wanted them to realize this is my house, and if they want to stay in it, they must do as I say. I don't allow smoking indoors and they must change their shoes.'

Peter thought of his own house on the other side of the town, with its overflowing ashtrays and unmade beds.

'I knew what I was doing,' said Peter, 'I don't think children ought to have to be grateful to anyone, not even to their own parents. I wanted my children to be tough, to be strong, to have strong characters. To enable them to cope with life. Babs is tough all right, a little tiger.'

He drove home, anxious and worried. He seemed to have felt like this, anxious and worried ever since they came down from Wales the first time.

The children were growing up. He knew he must expect it to be more difficult than in the past, when they were very small and had to do what big Uncle said. He felt sure this 'difficult' period the girls were going through, would eventually pass.

Linda met him in the hall. She had a ribbon in her hair and he could see the new dress he had bought for her birthday underneath the coat she had on.

'Can I go out, Uncle?' said Linda. She knew that he would let her go, provided he knew where she was going and what time she'd be back. 'I'm going to the cinema but may not be back until midnight.'

'Linda, I won't have it. You must be home not later than ten thirty, you know that!'

'But Uncle, Babs does . . .'

'Linda darling, you're quite right. I know what you mean about Babs. It seems unfair to you if I let her stay out. But I don't exactly "let" her, do I? All right, I'll speak to Babs again. I'll say it's not fair to Linda.' He thought of Babs as she'd looked on the two or three occasions when he'd tried by persuasion and then by force, to keep her from going out. She fought him like a wild cat, beside herself with rage.

He knew it was useless. He felt suddenly very tired. Linda kissed him and whispered: 'Uncle, it's all right.'

He went into the sitting-room to join the others, watching television. Paul had his legs stretched out and he nearly stumbled over them. He and Willy had an ashtray between them, already untidy with ash and dead matches, trickling over on to the polished table.

'Aren't you going to clear up that mess?' he said sharply. Paul struggled to his feet and sauntered out with the ashtray.

'You needn't look like that, Willy,' said Pam, 'can't you see Uncle's in a bad mood?'

The situation did not improve. Babs did try to placate

him now and then by returning home promptly by 10.30 pm.
He felt grateful each time she did this. He knew she was
going out 'with friends'. She went with young people into
pubs where they stood giggling for hours over a drink, which
the boys bought for the girls.

At 11 o'clock one night Babs telephoned: 'Please Uncle,
I'm staying with a girl friend at Purley, I hope you don't
mind but I've missed the last train.'

'I shan't have to mind, shall I Babs,' Peter said, 'if you're
staying with a friend, it's too late for you to come home now.'

He went wearily to his bedroom. It was a beautiful room,
hung with some of his own paintings. He often wondered
whether they were 'any good' or not. The ancient, mullioned
window overlooked rolling meadows. He had an old dark
wood four-poster bed for which he'd made his own pink
ruched frill all round it, with two candle-type lamps on either
side of the bedstead.

He couldn't sleep. He got up, went downstairs, lit a cigarette and read some passages from 'Hamlet' before he could
relax.

It seemed to him that it was perhaps after all more difficult
to bring up girls than boys, though he preferred girls.

One evening a few weeks later, Paul shouted: 'Uncle,
you're wanted . . . on the 'phone.'

He supposed it must be Babs again, asking to be allowed
to stay out late like last time. He hadn't seen her since the
previous day.

Peter picked up the receiver and heard a man's angry
voice: 'Haven't you more sense than to let a 15-year-old
girl roam the countryside alone at night?'

It was the Police . . . a village police station somewhere
in Hertfordshire, not far from the Great North Road.

'If you will let me explain,' Peter began . . . when the
voice interrupted.

'You'd better come at once to collect this girl. Disgraceful,
I think . . .'

The policeman hung up before Peter could speak again. He went into the sitting-room; the children were viewing.

'Shan't be long . . .' he tried to speak lightly. 'I'm going to collect Babs.'

'Okay Uncle darling,' Margaret said, 'I'll keep an eye . . .'

'Thank you Maggie.' He was grateful to Margaret who, unlike Babs and Linda, seemed to have no desire to go out at night. Sometimes she spent the evening with his sister Pamela. Margaret was working for Pamela at present, helping her with a small business venture.

It was very nearly a 70 mile journey right into Hertfordshire. He drove fast as he always did when he was alone.

When he arrived at the village police station, he saw a woman police officer struggling with Babs. Like a wild-cat, her silky red hair almost hiding her face, she twisted and writhed and spat in fury. The pretty white face was contorted with it. She would not look at Peter. He had seen her like this many times before, incoherent with rage and anger at being caught.

The sergeant-in-charge was more understanding now, as he explained what had happened. With another officer, they were patrolling the Great North Road in the fading light when they saw two young girls trying to hitchhike a lift from passing lorries.

'We always know,' the sergeant said, 'when we see a young girl at that time of night, on the highway, and no luggage, hitching a lift . . . it's trouble. And we always have to investigate.'

Babs in her fury, had refused to eat anything and refused to speak. But the girl who accompanied her—already returned to her home by the police—had explained that they'd decided quite suddenly, for no reason, to go to Scotland. To see the girl's grandmother who lived there.

So . . . it was just a stupid prank. To think that his Babs, could be so silly and bring disgrace upon the family, to go off like that without a word to anyone.

'All right then,' said the sergeant, 'we don't take too serious a view, you know. Young girls are always running away. But we'll have to inform the Authority. I believe this is your foster-child.'

Peter gave them the name of the Child Care Officer and said that he would also contact them. Babs sat in the back of the Estate car quite silent throughout the journey home.

In the following week, she stayed away from meals and refused to speak to anyone. She went out as usual and Peter didn't try to stop her. She came home at the correct time and, sulkily, went to bed.

Peter telephoned the Authority and asked them to suggest a school where Babs could go for some training and discipline. He knew now that he had to give up the struggle. He had failed with Babs. It was his first failure in the family. It hurt.

A strict convent school at Staplehurst was recommended by the Children's Department. A few days later, Peter drove her there and handed Babs over to the Mother Superior. It was a convent of nuns specially trained to impose a firm discipline on unruly girls. There would be no more running away. He said goodbye to the nuns and returned to Lovelocks Farm.

Margaret had laid the table for tea and put a bottle of wine ready for him. He didn't want anything to eat, he said, just the wine.

There was a rather gloomy atmosphere at meal times now. The girls tried to be tactful. 'Uncle', they told everyone, 'was in a bad mood.'

27

Terry

The trouble was that he missed Babs. She spent a year at the school. Peter went down on visiting days. Things began to improve. Babs did well at the school. At the end of the year, Babs had a party, to celebrate her 'passing out'. She was very excited. Her special guest was—Uncle.

Afterwards he drove her back to Lovelocks. He was glad to have her home. She was his child; they all were his. If they behaved badly, he couldn't stop them; but it could never alter anything for him. Even if they ill-used him, he would just have to put up with it because if you loved someone and gave to them, you didn't just stop giving. Or did you? Peter wondered. Where did you draw the line? Was there ever a line to draw? He didn't think there was and thought he must remember to ask Anne about this next time he saw her.

'You are too good I think,' Anne said. She really meant it. She felt she would never attain such spiritual grace.

'Perhaps I have given them a different life from the typical family,' Peter said. 'I've brought them up to a rather bohemian sort of life, but there's nothing wrong in that, is there? I wanted the children to have a sense of adventure. You see Anne, we're a travelled family. Backwards and forwards to Wales two or three times a year; all the journeys to Lourdes. I'm taking Margaret to Lourdes this year.'

The first time he'd taken the children to Lourdes had been way back when the family were still at Knighton Spinneys. He'd taken Terry and Pam. It had all been delightful. On the journey by boat and train, everyone had taken notice of his two beautiful children; the glamorous Pam and the handsome boy Terry with his fine hair and eyes. Terry had been his favourite then.

Only Terry wasn't his favourite any longer, Peter said

grimly. Anne thought that Terry was the kind of boy who needed a lot of attention. In the old days when Anne lived near, Terry was always running to her house, to be made a fuss of by Auntie Anne.

It was Terry's last term at school. Peter decided he would have to look round to see what job Terry could do. None of the children, except for Margaret, showed any intellectual abilities.

Anyway, first they would all go up to Wales for a wonderful holiday at Ystrad Hall.

On their return to Surrey, Terry who was now nearing 16 years of age, loafed about the house for some weeks.

It was Brian's birthday. Peter gave him some money to add to his earnings from the paper round he'd had all winter. With this money Brian bought a shining, brand new bicycle. Brian was delighted and Granny and everyone came to his birthday party, for which Peter made a cake with 15 candles on it.

Terry behaved rudely at high tea that evening. Every time anyone spoke, he interrupted and said something unpleasant. Peter said: 'Terry, if you can't behave yourself, please leave the room.'

This situation lasted for some weeks, until Peter asked the boy why he was behaving like this. Terry said he was upset because Brian had a new bike, because he, Terry, wanted a bike too.

Peter tried hard not to feel impatient with his former favourite. In the end he brought home a somewhat old-fashioned bicycle which he bought for 5/- in a sale; it was still in good working order. Terry said something sarcastic and refused even to look at it.

'Terry,' said Peter, 'you know I'd be only too happy to buy you a new bike but you've got to do something towards it, like Brian does. All this term, Brian's been getting up at six o'clock to do a paper round; he never missed once and never even had to be called in the morning.'

Terry said he couldn't run as fast as Brian which was true.

'But you won't even clean my car for me,' Peter said, 'I've told you if you do that, I'll pay you ten shillings.'

Terry said something which was clearly intended to be witty and wandered off. Peter was at a loss to know what to do. It would be better when Terry found a job of some kind; he was at the difficult between stage. Peter realized, however, that Terry was suffering because he was not getting all the attention he needed. If only Terry could study for a RADA course as he had once done. Clearly, this lad was destined for the stage. The only one who could control him now was Anne Spence. She gave him her whole attention and laughed, or pretended to, at his jokes and much-coloured accounts of his doings. Anne's house was, however, too far away from Lovelocks for Terry to go there. He didn't like long walks—though it was only about two miles away—and now that he and Uncle were at loggerheads, he didn't want to ask for a lift.

One day Peter was setting out to visit Auntie Anne. As he left the kitchen, Terry, having at last got out of bed, was coming downstairs.

'Wait for me Uncle,' Terry called, 'I want to come with you to see Auntie Anne.' Peter replied: 'No Terry, I can't take you—not now.'

Linda stepped into the hall. She knew, as all the children did, that Uncle was irritated and worried by Terry's behaviour.

'Stop it, Terry,' said Linda, 'you can't go with Uncle. Didn't you hear Uncle say that he has to go there by himself . . .'

Terry's temper flared and he gave Linda a savage push, as he tried to follow Peter through the hall. Linda lost her balance and fell headlong through the glass front door.

Linda screamed. For the first time in years, the children were frightened of what Peter would do. He picked up the screaming Linda and carried her to the kitchen. Both ankles were deeply cut and blood was streaming from the cuts which were still embedded with pieces of broken glass.

He sat the sobbing girl on top of the kitchen sink and painstakingly removed each piece of glass, while the children watched in silence. All the time, as he worked, he talked to Linda in a soothing voice:

'There little darling, that won't hurt much, it's all right, look, that bit's out now. And we'll pull the skin over the cut there . . . just like that so that if lies flat. We don't want any nasty bumps . . . don't cry darling, it's nearly over.'

He carefully dabbed each cut with witchhazel. She had no other cuts except on her ankles. He bandaged them and then carried her into the car. It was a hospital job now; she would need a score or more of stitches before the scars healed.

The children were still watching. They hadn't, he thought grimly, been as quiet and silent as this for a long, long time. He knew too what they were thinking. This was Linda who'd been seriously hurt, Linda, the favourite, whose every hurt seemed to hurt him too.

There was no sign of Terry.

When Peter had left with Linda for the hospital, Margaret went upstairs and opened the door to Terry's room. He was sitting on the bed. She saw that he was trembling so violently that even his teeth were chattering. Margaret said something but Terry didn't seem to hear. She said: 'Terry, you must apologize to Uncle.' The trembling continued and she closed the door and left him.

At the hospital out-patients' department, Peter said there had been an accident and the cuts in her ankles were stitched. The Sister praised Peter for his work. She said she was sure there would be no permanent scarring now.

In the days that followed, Terry behaved as though nothing had happened. He stopped coming to meals and instead he sat on his bed sulking.

Peter realized that Terry was trying to attract attention. Margaret said it would have been better if Uncle punished Terry for Linda's accident, but Peter refused even to refer to it. He felt bitter that Terry hadn't said a word of apology to him about it.

M

Peter discussed the whole affair with the family doctor who was highly qualified and had considerable experience in psychiatry as well as medicine. The doctor suggested it was clearly a case for psychiatric help and possibly for electric shock treatment. Peter went home and broke the news to Terry. Terry's expression was one of delight. 'Oh thank you, Uncle,' he said smiling.

Later Peter drove Terry to the County Hospital for his appointment. Terry was his normal, charming self, making witty conversation and laughing at his own jokes. He was polite and affable to Peter. He said: 'Uncle, did Linda tell you that I apologized to her?'

Linda had been very nice to him and told him not to worry because 'it was just an accident'.

'She would,' Peter said, 'my kind-hearted girl!'

On arrival at the hospital, Peter and Terry were taken for a consultation. The doctor in charge was much taken with Terry.

Later Peter was told he could leave Terry at the hospital for a day or two and they would look after him. 'What a delightful boy,' said Sister, 'I am sure we shall enjoy having him as a patient.'

Later Peter received a report on Terry's case. They were of the opinion that no treatment was necessary and that therefore the electric therapy suggested by the doctor was out of the question. The report said that Terry was a normal, healthy boy and not at all neurotic.

Peter was almost relieved when Terry decided he would like to go and live in London in a room of his own. The Authority agreed to this and Terry for a time took a job as an errand boy in Fleet Street, acting as runner for a newspaper.

They parted good friends and sometimes Terry came home and spent the weekend with the family. The Terry affair did, however, leave its mark on Peter.

He was saddened by it, even more than by the Babs affair.

The family had to grow up, of course, but he hadn't expected it to happen so soon and in this way.

Peter started to have splitting headaches, just like Babs had had as a child, when he carried her to his own room for comfort. He always enjoyed a glass of wine with his meal and he found this helped. Now there were often empty places round the table. Linda had her own friends now and was starting work soon. Paul didn't always come into meals. Besides it was usually the children now who did the talking. He just listened, unless someone asked him a question. They had so many things to do in the evenings so that often he was left sitting alone at the table, with just Denise and Brian and Christine. When he felt depressed, as he often did, he went to the sitting room, taking the remains of the wine with him. He always liked it, but now he was drinking more of it than ever before. He told himself often that this was bad and it must stop.

28

John

Some of the children called themselves by Peter's second name Lloyd, but all the children had at least one parent of their own.

John was the only one of the children in Peter's family who never had a birthday card or visit from a relative. John had no one.

One day when he was about 14 John had suddenly asked him: 'Uncle, where is my mother?'

The question worried Peter because he knew that the Authority also knew very little about John's origin.

Peter said: 'I don't know John. I think she must have gone away.'

John then said: 'Don't you know where she is? Doesn't anybody know?'

Peter told him that he supposed she could be found, but it would take some time.

It was one of Peter's special worries that John could not grasp the situation behind this. John stared at him and said:

'But it's not right Uncle. She's my mother. And I want to meet her. You must try and find her.'

Peter wrote to the Authority and explained the position. In the next two years, John often asked for news, but there was none. The Authority knew little except that a girl had placed the baby in their care and said that she was unmarried and had no home or means of her own. They had never heard from her again. For this reason John could not be offered for adoption, as this required the legal decision and signature of the parent.

Several years later, Peter was told by the Authority that they had managed to trace John's mother. She was working in a hotel in London. She did not want to meet John, but they had insisted. In the end, after some tears, she agreed.

A rendezvous was arranged on neutral ground. The mother wrote that she preferred to travel to Surrey rather than have John visit her. She said she had no 'place' of her own.

The meeting was to take place at the house of Anne Spence. Peter drove John there one Sunday afternoon. John was beside himself with excitement but Peter felt a chill foreboding.

The meeting was a fiasco, worse than he had feared. At first Anne busied herself handing round plates of dainty sandwiches and cakes which she and Helen had prepared. How did John's mother like her tea? With cream and sugar or just plain with milk?

John's eyes never left his mother's face, but she did not once look straight at the lad. She asked no questions. She did not ask what school he had attended or what sort of work he did now. She did not even ask who were these people, Anne and the pretty young Helen, Anne's eldest foster child, plying her with cakes, or the tall excessively handsome young man who had brought her and her son together.

John was too painfully eager to feel shy. He kept asking questions. Why hadn't they met before? Where did she live? How did she live? When could he see her again?

Peter watched and listened and suffered for the boy. He called the woman 'Mum' once or twice; it produced no reaction. She appeared quite indifferent. It was clear to Peter and Anne that she had no interest in John, no curiosity about him and no wish to prolong this interview one moment longer than she need.

At one point John burst out: 'Why? I don't understand.'

She turned towards him but she still did not look into his face. 'You must understand, John,' she said firmly, 'that I was left as a very young girl in a most difficult position. I had no money, no home and I had to make a living. Your father left me; I don't know where he went or what he did. No, I don't want to say any more about it. I want to forget.'

She spoke quite sincerely and truthfully. It was clear to Peter that she wished to pretend to herself that it had never happened. Peter felt this is why she would not look at John. He also noticed that the boy and his mother were very much alike in their limitations. This was not a clever woman but she was at this moment a determined one.

Tea was over and she asked to be taken back to the railway station. John asked for permission to write to her and she granted him this on condition that he did not try to come and see her.

John went into the hall to say goodbye to her. Peter said: 'I feared it would be like this. She doesn't want to know.'

Said Anne: 'I'm afraid John looks completely shattered. It would have been better if they'd never met.'

Back at home John said: 'Uncle I've GOT to see her again. Why wouldn't she talk to me properly?'

John wrote to her begging, just this once, to be allowed to see her alone and talk to her. To reassure her, he had told her about his plans to join the Army and she need have no fear that he would ever expect anything from her.

At last she agreed. John went by train to London and sat waiting for her in a restaurant as arranged. This time, the interview proved even more frustrating and John returned home bewildered and unhappy. A letter followed, saying that she had no interest in him and that it would be better for both of them if they never met again.

'Don't worry, old man,' said Peter, 'you've got a home here for always, you know that.'

'I don't understand it,' John kept repeating the same words he'd said as a young boy, 'she's *my* mother.'

'It's hard for you,' Peter said, 'you started with nothing. But remember, at least, you've got SOMEthing.'

John became sentimental at this. 'I know you're all I've got, Uncle. You're father and mother both.'

Shortly afterwards, Peter took John to an army training

unit in Wales. There was an interview with the Army recruiting sergeant, and John signed up in the army. Every leave he went home to Lovelocks, to his Uncle and the family, with about £50 army pay in his pocket and an arm-full of presents for everyone.

Peter told Anne: 'He seems to be getting over his disappointment. He's really a terribly nice person and he's got no bitterness against anyone.'

29

Willy

It was Willy's turn next to go sour on Uncle. Now that Willy was going on for 16, were the same problems developing as they had with his brother Terry a year earlier?

Only Willy was quite different. A slight, sensitive, quiet boy, he had always been overshadowed by the more striking Terry. Peter felt that Willy, like Christine, must feel more aware of being deprived than the other children. He was handed over to the Convent a few days after his birth.

Peter was also conscious that the 'failure', as he himself saw it, of the move to Wales affected Willy more deeply than the other children. He remembered Willy's white, stricken face on hearing the news at the dinner table that day in Ystrad Hall.

Since the return to Surrey, Willy became a changed person. Always a withdrawn child, he took on even more now the look of the 'lone wolf' who does not care for the company the world has to offer. There were distinct improvements in his moods every time the family returned on holiday to Llangollen, but in the few days before each return he became depressed. His greatest pleasure was to go salmon-fishing on the river and he was the only one of the children who liked to do it alone.

'You really love Wales, don't you Willy?' Peter once asked.

'Oh yes Uncle, I do.' Willy spread out his arms as though to embrace the distant hills. 'You see Uncle, no people.'

There were several incidents back at school in Horley. A fight or two, though Willy didn't want to talk about it. Then he left school and found a job as unskilled worker in a local factory, as the others had done. He became more and more restless and unhappy.

'You want to be on your own, don't you Willy?' said Peter.

This time he was determined to avoid trouble, to catch it in advance if he could.

'It's not that Uncle. I just don't like Horley.'

Willy became so disheartened and restless that finally it was agreed between himself and Peter that the Authority should be asked to find Willy a room of his own in London. This was arranged by a Miss Henderson of the Children's Department at County Hall, Wandsworth. Willy went to live with a friendly and helpful married couple and their daughter in Worcester Park. He also got a new job in the district.

This proved to be no solution to Willy's problems. It was some time before Peter saw Willy again. But when he did see him and hear his story, he realized that some problems are a case for experts, and Willy's certainly was. Willy's story, told by himself, also showed the Authority often showed a patience and understanding which went beyond that of a parent.

One day Willy, now nearly 18, turned up suddenly at Lovelocks Farm. He sat, hands on knees, and he did not look at Peter as his story came, haltingly at first.

'I soon left the couple and their daughter,' Willy said, 'I couldn't stand any more. They were the nicest people and they wanted to be kind and make much of me. But I didn't want it. I didn't want to be involved. No, Uncle, I don't know why. I just did. I don't trust people. I'm suspicious. I suppose I might have stayed if they'd left me quite alone, but they wanted to draw me into the family circle. I wanted to be just a lodger.' Willy glanced up at Peter, then stared at the floor again. He went on—in a monotone—with his story.

'So I walked out, leaving my luggage behind. I walked out of the job too. I had about three pounds on me. I just walked the streets. For about three weeks. Until my money was gone.

'I got in with some blokes who had drugs and that sort

of thing. I was on Methadrine and I went round with this crowd of boys and girls. I ended up sleeping on Paddington Station. I had nothing except the clothes I had on me. I got so fed up with everything; I was cracking up, not eating. I was with some fellows; we lived on sandwiches and tea. I started to crack up and I couldn't stand it any more.

'I rang up Miss Henderson at seven o'clock in the morning. At County Hall. You see, I didn't know what the time was. I didn't know anything; I was pretty paranoiac I think. At least, that's the word the psychy—psychiatrist or something—calls it, I think! Well, she wasn't there. So I kept ringing her for the next three hours, reversing the charges. Yes, they let you do that at County Hall. I was in this telephone booth and I couldn't hardly stand up. It was at East Putney. I didn't know how I got there, in a tube I expect.

'And I could hear people talking, and I thought God I was like a tramp. Miss Henderson came in a car and picked me up; I was still in this 'phone booth on East Putney Station. I said to her, "I'm in a state". She was rather angry; that is she told me afterwards that she was, but I couldn't take it in really. I went with her to County Hall, Wandsworth and I don't know . . . I must have been . . . I had cracked up by then. From there I went to Stamford House for two days, a sort of remand home; in the medical ward. I don't know what it was like; I didn't really know what was going on; they cleaned me up, gave me a bath; my hair was long; well after two days I came down to Horley. They let me go because I had got rid of the drug effects I suppose. I had a bob left. I just got on to a train. I still wasn't really with what was happening. I travelled on trains for several hours until I found myself at Horley. I gave the ticket man this bob and said I'd got on the station before. I went down to see Pat and Terry. (Pat was a friend of Babs.) They gave me a bed for a couple of nights. I didn't want to see you Uncle. I didn't want you to see me in the state I was in!'

Willy paused—lay back against the settee cushions and

for the first time he glanced straight at Peter as he went on with his story.

'Then I went back up to London to see Miss Henderson. We'd arranged that. I thumbed all the way to Streatham and from there I got another lift down to Wandsworth. I was so muddled up inside I started to talk to her. She asked me if I wanted to see a psychiatrist and I said yes. First she put me up in this Church Army House in Upper Richmond Road. I was still going round in a daydream. I saw a psychiatrist named Dr. O'Connell and he asked me if I'd like to go to his clinic, Northgate Clinic at Colindale. It's very nice. You have your own room and they give us Group Therapy. It's paid for on the National Health. You have patients all round and you're supposed to talk and if a patient says a problem, you mention your own and it might help you. It's very hard. I try to; only a couple of people can do it. I haven't spoken about my problem because I don't trust people in a group. My problem is people. It's suspicion mostly. I don't really know why I distrust people. I don't like crowds; I get scared of people. I have a psychologist and he listens. Therapy lasts three-quarters of an hour and then you have your own therapist and I can talk to him; I trust mine and I've got confidence in him, this Dr. O'Connell. Sometimes it lasts half an hour and sometimes two and a half hours. I'm going to leave soon and then I go to a place near Cambridge where they teach you to settle down in a job; it's a small village and they teach you to paint and that sort of thing.

'Yes, Uncle, you know I trust you. I didn't want to involve you Uncle. It's not just that I was ashamed of letting you down; it's a bit more than that. I didn't want you to know the sort of troubles I was having.

'I hate it when I see and hear people attacking you. I think that's terrible. I can't stand it. I know it's because other people are jealous of you, that they didn't have the ability or the patience to do what you did for us, Uncle. I've heard people attack you . . . you know why . . . because you're a bachelor. I tell people straight what you do or if they get too insulting, I hit them. It might not do them any good but it does me a bit of good. You had it organized; you knew what you were taking on. I know why you did it, because you were sick of seeing children with no homes and no one to lean on.

'You mustn't think Uncle that it hasn't worked out for me, because it HAS. Really it has. I've learned a lot from you, about values in people, all sorts of values. Even about money.

'The only thing I can't agree and forgive is bringing us back from Wales. Why did you do it? After living in Wales, in that beauty, I knew I never wanted to live anywhere else. Everything's spoiled after that.'

Peter listened to Willy's story, without speaking, right to the end. 'I think Willy, I spoiled it for everyone, including myself, by coming back from Wales.'

30

Paul

Willy had sat there on the settee in Peter's sitting-room and poured out his story with a sort of quiet release.

Afterwards Peter wondered if his own patience with the children could have harmed them. It had been one of the rules he made for himself to be patient with them always.

He recalled his after-dinner 'speeches' to them as they sat around the table. He told them that children had a right to speak their minds fearlessly; if they had something to say then 'out with it'. They were to treat him on equal terms and not be afraid. He wanted them in this way to learn to be strong and stand on their own feet. Even if they abused him, they were free to do so if they felt it right. He had been happy that they always came back, usually the same day, not to apologise but simply to say: 'Uncle, I was a bit bloody-minded about so-and-so but I had to get it off my chest.'

So, it occurred to him now, it may have been a shock to Willy to find that the outside world was not the same as Uncle's. He remembered Willy coming home from his first job and saying 'It's bloody awful, Uncle. They expect too much. And never a "please" or a "thank you".'

He told Willy that employers had rights too; that if he wanted to keep his job, then he couldn't very well argue with them or try telling them off.

Willy's words came back to him now.

'You're too patient, Uncle, that's the trouble. You should fight more . . . It's no use going on the way you do . . . You're the most bloody patient man I've ever met . . . but it's not the same outside . . . I never knew it was like that.'

It sounded like an accusation. Willy was saying, wasn't he, that Uncle had over-protected them. Was it true? Had he, even by omission, given the children a false impression of the world outside?

At present Peter was having a struggle to fight his own feelings of loss and depression. Really, he didn't know the answer and he suspected there might not even be one.

Anyway, he would try, he told himself, to be firmer with Paul. Paul was much less complex, or so Peter thought at first, than Terry and Willy. Paul's problem was quite simply that he could not get up in the mornings.

For several weeks Paul had a marvellous job as a builders' labourer working for Government contractors. They were laying pipes under the highway in the district and the pay of £15 to £20 a week was more than any of the children earned so far. The only snag was that the work started promptly at eight o'clock. For a little while Peter managed to remove Paul from his bed in time for work. It was all too good to last. Paul was fired in the end for being late for work.

A year went by and then nearly two. Paul had five jobs in that time but showed no enthusiasm for any of them. He almost seemed glad when he lost each one and could take to his bed again, sleeping excessively long hours as it seemed to Peter.

Yet Peter still hesitated, wondering how to deal with the situation. He was very fond of Paul; he admired his reticence and reserve, so different from the others' constant chatter; he liked his pleasing manner and good looks, his rueful candour and general 'niceness'. Peter sometimes felt that the half-innocent 'sinner' was already half-way to blessed goodness by the mere admission of sins. For this reason, he always expected that any day Paul's weaknesses would turn into shining virtues.

Time went by, however, and Paul did not improve.

Peter still tried whenever he saw Paul lounging about the house, to persuade him of his need to find something worthwhile to do with his life. Paul listened, eyes cast down, silky brown hair hiding his expression, which showed a

faint smile not so much mocking as admitting a fair amount
of contrition.

'After all,' Peter said, 'you must try to earn something
and contribute your share at least towards the hospitality
in the evenings.'

Peter was referring to the almost nightly 'parties' which all
the family gave for their friends. Peter himself often helped
by making endless pots of coffee and slicing scores of sandwiches. During the busiest year of all, the family and their
friends got through a regular weekly order, amongst other
things, of ten dozen eggs. The large sitting-room was kept
filled throughout the evening and often late into the night.
All the local youths and girls knew that it was Open House
at Lovelocks. And there weren't many like it in Horley.

Despite the crowd, Peter continued to occupy his own
chair in the sitting room every evening, often carefully
avoiding a dozen outstretched legs, or couples sitting on the
floor. It was quite common to find twenty-five young people
watching television in the sitting-room on a winter's evening.
Peter quite enjoyed these evenings because he could always
listen to the newest pop records with the same enthusiasm
as the youngsters. Anyway he liked them all. They were the
nicest people! Pam's boy friend and Christine's and Dink's.
And Linda's and Babs' in her time. Babs was back home
again and, clearly, glad to be. She was quieter and affectionate, though tough as ever. Babs now had a boy friend
even taller than Peter and how he suffered from the low
beams at Lovelocks.

Paul's friends also came. Sometimes they and Paul sat
drinking it the kitchen until, at last, Paul staggered slightly
drunkenly to bed. Next morning Paul slept late ...The days
and nights went by; litter and cigarette ends collected under
Paul's bed and across the floor of his room, and stayed
there ...

In the end, a little sickened, even Peter's soft heart hard-
ened and he turned Paul out of his room altogether, and
found him a place in the garden. This was not a mere

'hut' but a solid, small brick-built dwelling, once used as a store.

Peter, of course (because being Peter, he could not help himself), first painted part of the dwelling, installed electric light and laid a carpet on the floor, adding other necessary comforts. Paul's friends were thrilled with it and offered to decorate it throughout so that it could be turned into a cosy permanent 'den'.

The effect on Paul, however, was only to embitter him. Now he devoted his whole time to sleeping by day and spending the last of his money on drugs by night. In the end he was caught by the police with a stock of cannabis resin in his boot. He was fined. Most of his money from his next job went to pay the fine. This time he had even shocked himself. He gave up drugs and never touched them again.

One evening, returning from a journey to Hampshire, Peter met Paul in the hall and said he wanted to speak to him.

'Yes Uncle?'

'This time you have gone too far. You know I stick by you no matter what. But . . . scrounging money from the girls in the house . . . is too much!'

Paul said nothing. What was there to say?

'Worst of all,' Peter went on, 'this time your victim is Linda and heaven help the one who does the dirty on Linda. You know that?'

'I know, Uncle,' said Paul quietly.

'First you borrow 10/– from Babs. Apparently she is ready to speak up for you and I take that into account. She tells me you paid it back last Friday, sq good for you! But milking Linda with some stupid sob-story. That I won't stand.'

Paul still stood, silent, passive.

His stubborn, handsome face angered Peter. 'You can't go on forever making a fool out of me with your damn laziness and sponging on other people.'

In his whole life, Peter had never talked like this to anyone.

It took his own breath away, but he rushed on before his own fury would turn, as it nearly always did, into compassion.

'Don't you try to pull any more of this fast stuff,' Peter said. 'What right have you to borrow from Linda? You came to me with a sob-story on Sunday and asked for ten shillings. Then I find you have borrowed from Linda as well. How mean can you get? Linda's saving up to get married; she's got her own life and responsibilities; she can't afford to lend money to lazy wasters who haven't got the guts to work. I call it stealing, anyway, because you have no way of repaying it whatsoever.'

'I have, Uncle,' Paul said softly, knowing that if he could hold his own and fight back, he could still be the winner in this argument. Like all the children, he knew Uncle and knew that the furious words would stop and all would be the same in the end.

The trouble with Peter at that moment was that his anger would not or could not die down this time; simply because he knew that he was more angry with himself than with Paul. So THIS was what it had come to; this is what he wanted, wasn't it? He'd wanted the children, all of them, to be fighters! How could he have known it would come to this?

Linda came in and stood quietly by, uncertain what to do but waiting her moment to attempt a reconciliation between the two men.

Peter said: 'What do you need money for? You don't have to go anywhere. You get kept for nothing. What's it for?'

'Well, I need some for bus fares and for cigarettes,' said Paul in his mild and patient voice.

Peter could see the argument was getting nowhere.

'Give Linda her money at once,' Peter said. 'Two pounds I want from you.'

'When I get it, Uncle, I will!'

Paul already owed him over one hundred pounds, for Peter had been doling out money to him for his needs from

N

time to time. Even that time when Peter had to pay for a hair-cut so that he could go after a job. Paul always promised each time that he would pay his Uncle back eventually.

Paul left, slamming the door behind him.

The whole household was on edge after this latest episode. It was rare for Uncle to get so angry.

Linda tried to soothe him. 'It's not worth it Uncle, I don't mind about the money.'

Peter said: 'Everybody slams doors in this house. I wonder we've any doors left whole.'

Linda said she was sure Paul would pay her back as soon as he could.

Peter's mood changed immediately.

'Poor fellow, I feel sorry for Paul most of the time.'

Linda did not speak. She wondered if her Uncle whom she loved so much, as indeed they all did, realized that they ALL needed him and would continue to do so. Did he realize, too, that Uncle needed them all to need him?

More rows and arguments followed. Peter was suffering a great deal. It was so hard, even for him, to swallow the words he wanted to say as each day Paul came into the house, sat down at the table and waited to be fed.

Linda tried—they all did—to talk to Paul. Even one or two of the local girls came in the evenings, simply in the hope of seeing Paul.

Some members of the family took Paul's side from time to time against Uncle. Babs, for instance, who had 'been through it all once', was sympathetic.

Inevitably the trouble flared up again, over a trifling sum which Paul had 'borrowed' from one of the girls.

'Right, that's your lot,' said Peter, 'get out, and don't you ever borrow again from the girls in this house'.

The sudden smile on Paul's face was mainly due to nervousness but Peter saw it.

'It's all right for you to laugh at honour and pride and paying one's own way. I was brought up to believe that men who borrow from women are the lowest of the low, the scroungers, the meanest, and no men.'

Paul turned in the doorway. 'Oh mind your own bloody business, you great . . .' his last words were almost lost as he tore out of the house.

Later that night, Paul entered the sitting-room where Peter sat alone.

'Can I talk to you?' said Paul in a quiet voice. 'Please Uncle, can I talk to you?'

'Oh all right.' Peter sat down again; he felt exhausted, wordless at last.

'I'm sorry,' Paul said, 'I don't know what happened.'

'I suppose now you feel better, eh, now you've said your piece' Peter said: he sounded bitter. He was referring to the ugly name which Paul had used.

'Really sorry,' Paul went on, 'I don't know what came over me. I apologise for it . . . I even had to go to the Doctor after I left here, to give me something.'

'The Doctor? Whatever for?'

'To give me something for it. I felt terrible. I don't know how I came to say such things. I've never, to be fair "gone over the top" before Uncle, now have I?'

'No,' Peter said, 'on the contrary; you control your feelings well.'

It was impossible to distinguish whether this was sarcasm or not.

Paul went into the hall and brought back a bottle of Stout which Peter had left there earlier.

'Is this yours, Uncle?'

'Yes . . . I won it in a raffle.'

Paul spoke hesitantly. 'Can I . . . have it?'

Peter stared. Suddenly he burst out laughing. He laughed as though he could never stop. He felt he'd only just seen the joke. These children of his . . . how marvellous they were; really all that was needed was a sense of humour, he told himself. Why on earth hadn't he thought of it before?

N*

Paul was simply screamingly funny. Just like Babs and Willy and Terry and . . .

'Really I don't see why you should, after all your sweet words to me earlier on,' Peter said.

Paul said: 'I'll toss you for it.'

'You've got a nerve, you know! You tell me to "mind my own bloody business" and then ask for a free bottle of booze . . .!'

Paul tossed the coin, called 'heads' and heads it was Paul drank the bottle and then made for the door, carrying the oil-stove out to his 'den' in the garden.

Paul said: 'If only I'd been born rich; I might do all right.'

'No,' Peter said, 'it's a few more years of life you need. Things will work out in time.'

'I hope so.' Paul went out.

Peter sat there for a long time. He wanted to think about it; about his own feelings. What did he feel now?

He felt glad peace was restored. Then a thought suddenly occurred to him. If Paul did not exist, if he were not there in his house behaving shockingly badly, what then?

Then there would be no Uncle, would there? He, the big Uncle, experienced in the lessons of life, would be sitting there talking . . . to whom? To the wall.

Yes, it was quite clear that Paul could not do without his Uncle. But would Uncle's life be the same without Paul?

31

Linda

Peter was now convinced that growing-up was a most painful business. Those awful years from 15 to 19: he wondered how Kevin was managing.

One day Linda's father arrived to say he now had a nice house and would like the three children, Linda, Denise and Kevin to return to him. Linda and Denise refused, saying they wanted to stay with Uncle, but Kevin went. Peter was sorry to see him go; a quiet, sweet boy who gave no trouble. A little elf of a boy. How odd that when a child gave positively no trouble at all, somehow that child came to be overlooked. Was it too dull then, to have a no-trouble child? Peter thought this one over and failed to decide. Anyway, he was sorry to lose little Kevin.

The children had grown up so fast. By law, Peter knew he had no obligation whatsoever to keep any of the children once they had reached 18 years of age. They could leave any time they wanted to after that age; indeed he even had the right to chase them out, if he felt like it.

Well, he just hoped that some would want to stay even longer than that.

One day, hearing shouts and screams, he dashed upstairs to find Babs and Linda locked in a scuffle. Peter didn't waste time trying to find out what it was about. He clove his way in among the flailing arms and legs, the red hair and the brown. After the melée, Babs lay half-dazed on the floor. She sat up, feeling her chin carefully.

'You bugger!' said Babs.

But Peter was no longer there.

It was a shock when some months later Linda told Peter she wanted to marry a local boy. Peter knew the boy quite well from all the family evening parties when he'd been a regular visitor, and liked him very much. But as an agricultural worker he wasn't earning much. Peter felt it was certainly not enough to keep his Linda.

'But Linda darling you're only 16. Why? And where will you live?'

'I know Uncle, you always said you could never understand why girls like boys. Well, I like him Uncle, please.'

There was nothing further to say. He knew very well that even on their joint wages, they would never have enough money in the near future to be able to put down a deposit on a house.

Peter started to turn three of his upstairs rooms into a proper flat for the couple.

Before he could start making arrangements for the wedding, however, permission had to be obtained from Linda's parents. Her father consented.

Soon the family would be taking their holiday in Wales. The whole thing was now too expensive to maintain. Peter had sold Ystrad Hall to a man who wanted to turn it into a residential home and with the money he was able, finally, to clear his debt with the Bank. It was a relief because the cost of maintaining the family at Lovelocks was mounting each year. It wasn't easy to economize, Peter found. The family were used to a high standard of living and he, for one, would not want it otherwise.

He was able to get through the days without thinking too much because once again there was a great deal to do. Everything must be arranged for the wedding and the attic flat must be equipped and made ready for the couple as soon as they returned.

Linda's bedroom was up there, three flights up. He now took over the two adjoining rooms and started to instal new electricity and water supplies, so that it would become a complete and separate living area. As always, he did all the work himself; it meant bowing double and squeezing his great frame through two small doors two feet high and 18 inches wide. Then he had to do the work inside a roof-space in a corridor two feet by three feet by about 50 feet long. There he connected cold water pipes and drains and electric cables. He made about 16 visits into this tiny space, because sometimes he forgot to switch something on or off. Back he went with a box of tools which were easy to lose in that total darkness. He reminded himself once again that he was just like Alice in Wonderland when she grew and grew and the walls stayed as they were.

He fitted a sink heater and then painted the attic, made curtains for the whole 'apartment', followed this by making a row of fitted cupboards. He managed to get it all completely furnished in time for the wedding.

The following year when the baby came, Peter fitted a gate at the head of the steep stairs and wired a doorbell from the bottom. He fitted an inter-com from the family kitchen downstairs up to Linda's sitting-room so that whenever the couple were wanted on the telephone or by a friend or tradesman, they could easily be called. Every day he thought of a new idea for making them comfortable.

Meanwhile they put their names down on the local housing list and everything went on as before. Linda's young husband returned from work each day via the family back door where Linda, using the family kitchen, had his dinner ready as he came in. Peter did not think it was safe for cooking to be done upstairs in an all-wooden attic.

Peter felt more cheerful as things settled down again after the upheaval. He was thankful he had got this place which he could convert for them. Better than having to worry how and where they could live. How he'd have hated Linda having to live in a caravan like so many of her friends. They could have hardly lived with her in-laws who had only a tiny house.

One day some months later, he was sitting at his desk. Keeping the books was a job he hated. Each day he sat down to try and keep up to date in controlling the budgets for three families' financial needs. He paid all the overheads for the house and family of Anne Spence (and the third family run by Patricia).

He didn't like the dull arithmetic of it, but he enjoyed his place at the head of the household. He hoped he looked solid enough for the job, like a responsible Victorian father for instance. If the children would leave him in peace, he might get the paper work done for today.

Suddenly the door opened and Babs came into the room. Babs was living at this time in a small flat in a nearby town, having found a good job as a waitress in a cafe just opposite her lodgings. She was having, Peter heard from the rest of the family who'd visited the cafe as customers, something of a success. The customers liked the red hair, the sparkling looks, and the wit. Babs could always make people laugh.

'Uncle . . . I've got something to tell you!'

'What is it?' Peter said, hoping she would go away if she saw that he was really busy with serious matters.

'Um' said Babs, 'er!'

Peter looked up. 'Got kicked out of your flat, then?'

'No!' Babs said. Her smile was sheepish though.

'Do you need some money then?' Babs shook her head.

'Had a row with the boy friend?' Peter knew Chris who was a regular visitor.

'No!'

Peter knew Babs rather well, or thought he did. In spite of the fierce rows they'd had in the past seven years, he liked her. More than that. Like all the children, she was special to him. She had spirit; he admired that.

'Is it personal then? All right then. Sit down,' said Peter. Babs sat.

'So when are you getting married?' Peter was becoming very worldly-wise. Babs laughed, a bit embarrassed.

'Well . . . I don't know yet.'

'Don't hedge Babs . . . it's not like you.'

Babs said nothing.

Peter swivelled round on his chair, looked at his desk calendar and counted out four weeks.

'All right, February 10th, that's the day.'

He pencilled the date round on the calendar.

'That's it then,' Peter said.

'If we must Uncle, we'll do as you say. It's not that we don't want the baby. We intended to live together. But marriage! All that rigmarole; it's just not up our street.'

'I think it will be better for the baby, to make it official . . . and keep the books tidy for the Registrar.'

'Just as you say Uncle.'

'And where shall you live?'

'Ah,' said Babs.

'Meaning you haven't anywhere,' said Peter.

'Please can we come to you Uncle, we've no money.'

Peter thought. He had been working on several of the upstairs rooms in order to make a self-contained apartment for himself.

If he gave this up, there would be an extra flat and he could let Linda choose whether to move into the apartment he'd made for himself or stay where she was and let Babs have it.

He looked at Babs. Heaven knows, she'd given him trouble enough already. On the other hand if he refused her, where could she go?

He knew thousands of other young couples were in the same condition. Rooms advertised were always at rents they could not afford and in any case had no space for children. Many plainly stated 'no children'. Sometimes there were a few houses to let, but never at less than ten to twelve guineas a week.

The neighbours would soon get to know that Babs was pregnant. When he took her shopping with him, there would be those curious, hard stares he well remembered from that tormented time in the house called Knighton Spinneys. There would be people who would grin or sneer or gossip. So be it.

'All right Babs, you can come to us. After all this is your

home. Where else should you go? We'll ask Linda which
flat she prefers; the one I was making for myself or the one
she's in now.'

'Thank you Uncle darling, you're an angel. I knew you'd
say yes.'

Babs hugged him quickly and went from the room. Not
that Babs had had the slightest doubt when she entered the
room, that Uncle would take her back. Then she remembered
something and opened his door again.

'That old radio set, you don't want it any more, do you
Uncle darling. Can we have it for our new home, and that
old television set you said you were going to have to throw
out?'

Peter was working out on paper how he was going to
re-arrange the house. He nodded to her; 'All right Babs,
take what you want, and let me get on with it now.'

Babs lost no time in consulting Linda who was delighted
at the prospect of moving into Uncle's own apartment which
was larger and more self-contained than the present one.
Peter was told the girls had made their choice. Linda would
move into his new flat immediately and Babs would move
into Linda's.

Peter felt a pang in his heart when he heard the news.
It was not because he was losing his own place though this
was a setback. He'd planned, now the children were growing
up and there was little real work for him to do, to retreat
into his own privacy and perhaps continue with his painting.
He liked to practise singing alone in the evening, to the
accompaniment of a Frank Sinatra record with Frank's
voice turned down low. He was also composing some music
of his own. He might even write a Musical, he thought one
day, and set the long adventures of being only an Uncle to
his own composition.

The pang he felt was because Linda was ready to give up,
eagerly and without hesitation, the nest he had worked and
lovingly furnished and painted specially for her. He said
nothing, however.

The rooms in her flat had belonged to herself and Pam for the previous two years. They had a view over the garden right down to the woods half a mile away across the two paddocks belonging to the property. The high wall beneath Linda's window was covered in wisteria and outside the other smaller window was a beautiful copper beech which almost seemed to Peter, to peep into her bedroom. How happily he had fitted a 13 amp socket for her electric fire of the wood-surround variety and another one for the record player which he was giving the couple as a wedding present. He'd connected additional ceiling lights to her bedroom with pendant switches each side of the bed, or at least over the position where their double bed would be placed when it arrived. To convert the kitchen he'd bought from some friendly builders, an enamelled sink-top with left-hand drainer and built a kitchen cabinet beneath using two-inch by five-eights deal with sides rigid and strong in heavy, veneered blockboard. Then he made sliding doors on nylon runners and over the sink he fitted a Creda hot water boiler, the seven-pint capacity with a 2500 watt element. He built a five-door kitchen cabinet, running the full length of one wall, about six feet long, fitted rows of shelves and had formica cut into special shapes to fit them. Finally, he bought 30 feet of half-inch copper pipe for her water supply . . . He remembered the hours of work, crouched double in the narrow space behind the old walls. In all, he reckoned to have done and installed not less than £250 worth of home comforts which cost him only about £100. He painted the apartment throughout in Linda's favourite shade of lilac.

Now she was giving it all up to Babs! His heart ached at this. Linda? Was she too like the others, calmly oblivious to his feelings?

Peter was helping with the removal from one flat to another when someone came in with the news that Margaret was leaving.

32

Margaret

For the past two years Margaret dreamed of going to America. It was Margaret's habit always to dream aloud. All the family knew therefore that Margaret was pining to see what it was like over There.

Peter felt as weary as though he'd been all the way there on foot and back again, simply from exhaustion at hearing Margaret talk about it.

The others who didn't have the energy even for thinking about such long expeditions, simply said that Margaret was a nag.

'Now what's old Fat-guts on about?' Paul said. Margaret had a charming roundness to her limbs unlike the slighter Babs or the frail Christine or Pam. They referred to her as Moo-cow or Fat-guts but Margaret had held a shorthand-typing job in London for a time, and could afford to ignore the 'peasants', as she called them, of Lovelocks Farm.

'Uncle darling,' Margaret said, 'you *did* say I could go. You said if I stayed in my last job for eighteen months, then I could go to America after that.'

'Well it was an improvement on your previous jobs which you held for four weeks or so at a time,' said Peter.

'Uncle I would like to go . . . just to have a look. I wouldn't stay longer than a year. I'd be too homesick after that.'

'I suppose you could go,' Peter said.

'How can I find out about jobs?' asked Margaret who knew perfectly well, just as Babs and Linda and Pam and all likewise knew, that having stated what they wanted, they could sit back and let Uncle do the rest.

'I'll look up a suitable Agency for you', Peter said, 'if you're really serious.'

He pointed out that America didn't want people who left

their jobs after four weeks and looked to the State to support them.

'Oh I wouldn't do that, Uncle,' Margaret said.

'Supposing you don't like it?'

'I'd like a job ... say, looking after children, please Uncle. Will you write to an Agency for me then Uncle dear?'

'All right then,' said Peter, getting up from his chair, in the knowledge that he would be asked once every two hours at least as to whether he had posted the letter to the Agency or not.

'Oh thank you Uncle,' said Margaret, giving him a playfully passionate hug.

Unlike her sister Babs, who started to drop her 'aitches' once she'd left school, and unlike all his other girls, who still spoke a relentless Cockney Margaret was well-spoken, had grammar and grace with a certain sophistication.

He realized the futility of asking her if it were wise to go so far from home, with the little experience of life she had had so far. Besides Peter felt convinced that wisdom was something born not out of successes, but out of failures. He looked up a good Agency and wrote them immediately about Margaret's wish to go West. He suggested she could fill a job as Mother's Help.

Margaret chose a job from among those offered, to go to a large family where there were seven or eight children, a large house, other staff and, according to the details given by the Agency, a 'busy, bustling family life'.

To Peter this sounded ideal because it would be the sort of life to which Margaret was accustomed.

'Do you like the idea still, Maggie? Have you any doubts about it?'

Peter, despite nearly a decade's experience, still held girls and women in profound 19th-century esteem. Girls were for protecting by men or whatever. Girls belonged, in Peter's eyes, in a Henry James novel or a Charles Morgan or Gene Stratton Porter one. Combing out Pam's beautiful long golden hair, as he'd always done before school in the old days, he saw them all as 'Little Women', unchanged since the days of Louisa M. Alcott.

'No doubts at all,' said Margaret. 'This job sounds just fine to me.'

Peter said: 'I certainly think it's the kind of thing you would do best—working in a large family. The older ones are just about your age anyway and this would give you a good chance to get to know them.'

Margaret's fare across was to be paid by her employer, as is customary. She would have to pay her own fare for the return journey and to ensure this, her employer would deduct an amount from her wages each week to cover the fare and give it to her when she left. Peter was satisfied with these arrangements.

Peter realized that getting a permit to work in the United States was no simple matter. However, his patience and Margaret's were quite exhausted long before all the formalities were done. There was a great deal of paper work and health checks and injections and visas to be obtained.

In fact, the formalities took so long that by the time all was complete and Margaret ready to leave, her future employer had already had her new baby and found somebody else to take Margaret's job. Margaret had to find a post elsewhere when she got there.

It was a bad beginning, but things got worse for Margaret who found the only job available was in a household with one child in Boston. Margaret pined. She was too much the 'lady' to do as Babs might have done and gone out on her hours off to look for company, even if it were only a giggle over a coffee in a drugstore.

After all the nerve-wracking preparations and Margaret's non-stop commentary on all concerned, Peter was resting at home in what felt to him like a sea of calm after the storm. However, it was not for nothing he had trained his children how to behave if a storm came up while they were lost on Kitchen Mountain at Llangollen. Always to telephone and reverse the charge. This Margaret did, for several months until the 'phone bill reached nearly £200 and Peter decided it would be cheaper to send Margaret the fare to come home again.

'I'm not happy Uncle darling. I hate it Uncle. I'm so lonely Uncle. I'm homesick Uncle darling. There's no one here to talk to Uncle, so I have to keep talking to you over the Transatlantic 'phone. Please don't hang up Uncle darling, I've got lots more to say.'

Peter sent Margaret the necessary £100 for a sailing ticket home and drove to the coast to meet a tearful Margaret who threw herself into his arms. Peter put her in the car and sighed happily. They couldn't do without him; none of them. Poor little Maggie, he said smiling. Uncle did have his own very solid place in their lives after all, he felt.

33

Pam and Christine

Despite so many departures in these tormented, teenage years of the family, the house seemed more crowded than ever.

For one thing, there was Angela, Linda's beautiful little daughter. Peter was happy to baby-sit when Linda and her husband went out for the evening. Sometimes he felt that out of all the children, Angela was his favourite of all. Nor did Linda have to worry if the baby's nappy needed changing or if the baby's wind was troublesome. Peter never had to ask advice from anyone; he always knew what to do.

Babs and husband were comfortably installed in Linda's former flat. Paul's big sister, Sandra, occupied Margaret's old room for a while, and a little boy named Simon who, like John, had no one, came to live with the family. Just to keep things ticking over, Peter supposed but he didn't feel quite sure about it. Like any proper 'mother', he felt he'd given his youth to his family, his own twelve dear children and was hardly in the mood to start again. However, Simon stayed since no one could think of a reason why he should not.

There was also most Sunday evenings nowadays, a visit from the father of Pam and Christine. The good, kindly man had long since recovered from his bitter disappointment at losing his daughters to Uncle. He came frequently and ate with the family and sat and viewed television with them.

Pam and Christine showed him affection, welcomed him and then went out for the evening with their regular boy-friends, leaving their father to doze in his armchair before the fire.

Peter's 'guilty' feeling towards the man ensured that he

always made him doubly welcome. Yet, Peter reflected, if all parents of children in someone else's care acted throughout in such a trusting, friendly manner, life for foster parents would be so much easier. There was, however, not much conversation between them, once Pam and Christine had greeted him.

'Hallo Dad, how are you?'

'Fine Pam. Hallo Christine, how are my girls?'

'We're fine, father.'

'I'm going out with Tommy tonight, Dad.'

'You go along Pam, do as you please. Who's Tommy?'

'We're engaged Dad, we're going to get married as soon as we can.'

'Oh you are, are you? Ah well.'

The girls left with their escorts. Their father tried to keep awake but sleep overcame him.

'He does shift work, you know,' Peter told Brian, 'Poor man, he must get very tired. Coming all this way during his hours off.'

Pam's father opened his eyes. To Peter he said: 'This fellow Pam's fallen for; seems a nice chap. But why do all the girls go for this long hair? Boys with long hair; I suppose I'm just a square.'

He dozed off to sleep again, waking a few hours later to drive back alone to London.

Pam returned at a reasonable hour—she had none of Babs' wildness—in time to give a drink and a cuddle to her two miniature poodles, soft, woolly, pretty creatures whom she adored.

Peter was relieved to see that Paul was improving. He had a job in a factory and was now contributing a few pounds a week towards his keep. Relations between them were now friendly. Paul seemed quite happy to stay at home as much as possible and became helpful in cleaning the kitchen and doing the washing-up. His own room, however, stayed as untidy as ever.

Margaret had decided to 'lead her own life' in a flat in

London. She persuaded Peter to find her a flat, to provide some of the necessities for it and to pay a substantial subsidy towards the rent, at least for the first year, until she could establish herself.

'I'll pay you back Uncle one day, you know I will,' Margaret said.

Brian said: 'Maggie, would you like a rare painting to hang on the wall in your new flat. Uncle said it's a bit bare.'

'Watch it Moo-cow,' said Paul, 'someone in the village has been flogging his works of art to Brian.'

Brian who now had a good job as apprentice in a factory was earning more than any of the family. However, he kept all of it to himself after paying Peter several pounds a week towards his keep, on the understanding that he wanted to save up enough money to go and find a place of his own one day. In fact, he had many suggestions to make to Peter about it being time for the family to move again.

'Well you said yourself Uncle, it's getting a bit crowded again.'

'That's true,' Peter said, 'but remember I took this house on purpose to last out until everyone was old enough to fly away if they wanted to.'

'Well,' Brian said, 'that'll be when Christine is 18 and she's not 15 until November. Don't know where I'll be . . .'

'Anything could happen in three years,' Peter said. 'Just think of the changes since we came here—Linda married, Babs married, Margaret with her own flat in London, Willy in digs . . .'

'Will they pull the house down when we go?' Brian asked.

'Brian,' said Paul, 'is planning to go into the property development business, in case you hadn't guessed.'

'Oh lay off,' said Brian.

Peter said he believed the Council's plan was to develop the land if they could get planning permission and then the house would be demolished.

'Judging by the holes in the roof, I wouldn't be surprised

to see the roof take off in a high wind. It seemed in such wonderful condition when I first looked round it. Of course, it is very old; the middle part almost certainly 15th-century, which makes it nearly five hundred years. Just a tiny part of it anyway.'

'What, my bedroom and the part underneath!' said Brian, with a gleam in his eye. 'I say, if I took up the floorboards, d'you think I might find some ancient stuff? It fetches a high price at those antique shops.'

Recent floods had damaged the house, destroying the electric motor and pump of the central heating and hot water system.

'I expect it's a hundred years since the house last stood in water,' Peter said, 'and the effect would probably be that the soil immediately underneath the foundations must be saturated. So the house won't really dry out till next summer. That's why there's a gradual rise of damp up one wall after another.'

However, the family entertaining continued as before, damp walls or not. In the village, the family friends would say to each other: 'Let's go down to Lloydsville.' They arrived at seven o'clock and stayed until 10.30 pm, except for Fridays and Saturdays. Then they could stay late and many stayed to watch the Midnight Movie on BBC-2 and went home in the morning dark. These parties drank upwards of 25s worth of coffee a week and consumed vast quantities of mixed sandwiches. A 20-minute gap was permitted for the girls to say goodnight to their boys, if they were courting or 'going out' regularly. Peter rather liked them; nearly all were courteous enough to say 'good evening' to him even if they hadn't met him before. Anyone was permitted to go into the kitchen and cook a snack or make coffee if they felt like it.

Sometimes the noise of their scooters going home on late nights caused a disturbance, but Peter was able to resolve this problem by making it a rule that they must push their bikes right down to the end of the road, before starting up the engine.

The parties had become smaller in the past year, since Linda's and Babs' weddings, but somehow the house was always overflowing. Each morning he noted with rising irritation that there were two dozen coffee mugs standing unwashed in the sink—despite the new dishwasher he had bought and which stood there unused.

Meanwhile, Peter was working on a new room of her own for Pam. He made her a dressing-table by covering a slate-shelved larder in the room with foam-backed pink material laid over it. He put in wall lights and painted it throughout including the old store cupboards where Pam could hang her clothes. It was too small and low-ceilinged for Peter to stand up in it, but Pam was delighted.

If only he didn't always feel tired these days, and a trifle depressed though he didn't know why he should be. Perhaps it was all the extra work due to the floods having destroyed a wood-block floor and a score of new holes appearing in the roof. With two babies now living in the house, he would have to see to it himself rather than wait for the local builders who might never come at all.

Babs came into the sitting-room. The family were viewing. 'Uncle . . . I'm very sorry . . .'

'What about,' said Peter, sensing trouble when Babs said she was sorry about something.

'I only put it down the same as I always do, Uncle.'

'Put what down, dear?' said Peter, keeping one eye firmly on the television.

'The toilet seat.'

'And it broke, you mean?'

'No . . . IT didn't break!'

'What do you mean . . . IT didn't break? Something broke, you mean, or fell off, or broke a cup or something?' Peter was watching the screen quite fervently now, in the hope that whatever the trouble was, it would go away.

'The toilet broke . . . it just fell to bits . . . Honest, all I did was put the seat down?'

Peter surprised himself by saying calmly: 'Never mind.'

'What shall I do Uncle?'

'I'll look at it tomorrow. Everyone had better use the one in the hall. I don't think we need put a notice in the bathroom to say the other one's broken, do you?'

'It certainly *looks* obvious enough . . . it's all over the floor . . . the bits. I mean . . . the . . . er . . . oh you know, the china stuff!'

The 'one in the hall' had been kept till now for visitors and so on, because it was rather out of the way for people upstairs and on the top floor. Now, Peter realized, it meant that everyone would have to troop downstairs for days and nights, and from the attic flat as well, until this one was repaired.

Peter informed the plumber next day, but three weeks later the man had still not arrived to inspect the site. Peter was fed up, as so was everyone else, with the endless traffic downstairs, so he bought a new pan and fitted it himself. Normally he enjoyed plumbing and electrical work, especially fitting copper pipes because he thought copper a beautiful metal and he loved the smell of linseed in Boss White with the brass fittings so superbly made to hold the whole thing together.

But this time he couldn't really say he enjoyed the job. Fitting a new pan was no picnic for an amateur and the surrounding air from a gaping and ancient soil pipe was neither bracing nor stimulating to him. He spent several days on his knees cutting, plugging, levelling and connection pipes, taps, ball-cock and overflow, adding a new seat to give tone to the whole enterprise. Still, he was glad to stand upright again and accept the compliments of the first visitor to use the sparkling new object.

Brian who hung around quite a lot of the time to see what was going on, said: 'Well done.' Brian was known not only for his fondness for trading and swops and deals. He also liked to act as Inspector when a job of work was being done. Brian, Peter thought, was destined for some kind of inspection work though he always wished Brian would go and inspect somewhere else, declaring that it made him nervous to have Brian constantly checking up on his activities.

Nevertheless, his cry of 'well done!' brought the rest of the family to join in the triumphal inspection. And not a moment too soon, alas, for the report arrived immediately that 'the other one' downstairs, after coping all alone with the inhabitants of three floors, had at that very hour rebelled, choked and finally failed altogether. Peter went wearily downstairs to apply the dismal notice on its door 'Closed!'

The house was still without hot water since the flood damage and next day Peter went hunting for plumbing ware and fitted a hot water cylinder in the bathroom and connected the mains to its immersion heater. It meant another session of stooping and climbing and he finally fell into bed, too worn out even to bother about the choked WC downstairs.

All the family were working now, except for Denise who had decided to stay at home and look after the housework and at least one meal a day for the family. She would earn her keep in this way and also act as daily baby-sitter for Babs' baby so that Babs could go out to work and earn some money.

Peter was glad that Denise did not have to face the 'world outside'.

It was enough that so many members of the family had already faced the world and been disappointed by it. And he felt this was only another sign of the happiness they'd enjoyed at home with him; especially their life at Ystrad Hall in Wales.

This had its bad side, admittedly—this 'happiness' at home. He remembered his own boyhood; at all times protected, never allowed out 'on to the streets'. He remembered how it came almost as a shock to go to prep school at nearly ten years old and meet other boys 'en masse' for the first time.

Denise was happy to stay at home and earn £4 a week for keeping house. Peter enjoyed her company and sometimes confided his troubles to her. As a child, she, like Margaret, sulked for days on end but she was more level-headed than Margaret and always ready to take a realistic view of life. Denise was a pretty, tiny rounded figure with beautiful legs, who looked so young for her age that Peter gave her a note to carry in her handbag with sworn evidence of her birth date.

Peter had done everything he could to strengthen Denise's 'bad arm'. When she slept in a bunk bed with the other children at Knighton Spinneys, he trained her to do 'pull-ups' by holding on to the springs above her. Peter played games with her to force her to use the arm; he tried to make her hit him by swinging her bad arm, which ran around loose on its own. He forced her into many a clenching competition when he made her grip his hand or arm with her 'bad one'. In the end the bad arm became so strong that it could often out-do the good one.

34

Peter and the Grown-ups

Suddenly it seemed his work was done and Peter did not know which way to turn. He never expected it all to happen so quickly.

His position now, he felt, was very much like that of a middle-aged housewife whose work of bringing up her family was done. For nearly ten years, his days and nights had been filled with exhausting work, with problems and work, with worries and work. Yet looking back, those years were the happiest when he stood at the washing-machine, throwing twelve white blouses and twenty-four little boys' shirts into it every Tuesday ... all those back-breaking Thursdays standing at the ironing board; were so much better than this; this emptiness. He thought of them almost with longing. He suffered bouts of depression, sometimes drank too much wine; contracted a scalp irritation which the Doctor explained as 'nerves'. He did not know how to fill the days. Throughout the most disturbing year of 1967/8 when Linda and Babs and their husbands and babies had to be housed, with Christine's 15th birthday which was a sort of landmark as she was the 'baby', he did not have time for the kind of thoughts which troubled him now. There had been the floods and the lavatory pans to mend and more repairs to the roof and more doing-over of rooms and wood-block floors; there had been no time for backward looks or introspection.

That Christmas had been the most grown-up he could recall. He served the children Dubonnet instead of pepsi-cola and gave them presents of money instead of hanging up the stockings.

Well, he would have to take stock; to examine his position with a view to a re-entry into the society of adult business people. But how? Where? What?

Now and then he made desperate sorties into the adult world again to try and make contact with former friends and acquaintances. Each time he returned home with relief to Lovelocks Farm, to Denise and Linda's baby daughter. He had to force himself to make the effort to go out and meet people and each retreat brought on a depression because of the knowledge that next time would be harder still.

He fell back on the resources still available. He drove one of Anne's children to hospital for treatment each day and spent a lot of time helping Linda with her work, on the pretext that she was now expecting another child and needed help. He took her shopping in his car and spent the rest of the time finding repair work still to be done in the house itself.

Now, when meeting people either locally or on rare visits to London, he was handicapped by a notion that he was a Rip Van Winkle alone and uneasy among strangers. He He told himself this feeling was due to his long isolation from grown-up society and that it had been necessary so that he could devote himself to the children's upbringing.

Once he went to London and, on an impulse, took a large expensive apartment in exclusive Arlington House. He bought flowers for it from Fortnum and Mason close by. The man who had bought the children's beds and furniture from Harrods was almost unconsciously trying to resume the role he'd abandoned ten years earlier. It was the role of man-about-town with a classic Rolls to drive, money in his pocket, a home in the country, membership of a good Catholic society and his name on the lists of a dozen or more distinguished charities.

He gave up the apartment six months later when he realized that he probably never would use or occupy it. Even on those evenings he found himself there, he often decided, perhaps as late as 10.30 or 11 o'clock, to get into the car and drive back to Lovelocks.

Yet he felt it as a defeat and blamed himself for his weakness.

'I find I miss,' he told Denise, 'the cosiness of family life.'

There, at the head of his large, thriving, growing house-hold, he'd had his place. Now he had none. They no longer needed him. At least, not as much. Not in the same urgent way.

Nevertheless, that last New Year's Eve, he had made a resolution to return to the business world, to return to social life, dining out, going to theatres, meeting people. And he was never a man to give in easily.

The effort, however, was, he felt, killing and he began to rely on Denise and Margaret to push him in the direction he wanted, unwillingly, to go.

He started to keep a diary to record his success and failure, including the comments and encouragement from the two girls. It was strange that he, on whom they had relied, for all comfort and strength, now needed them desperately for his own support.

He busied himself writing political articles on various themes. His diary noted: 'Where is the determination? I seem to have none. It seems true what Margaret and I said last night, that the comfort and cosiness of home life is too cosy to leave. I told Margaret that perhaps I lack courage.'

Margaret got into the habit of telephoning him several times daily to see what he was doing and to urge him on.

Underlying this was the knowledge that even now he could barely bring himself to face, that he was dogged by a sense of failure.

He faced for the first time in his life the fact that perhaps he had sought a life among children in order to avoid the harder problem of a life among adults. Margaret had once laughingly called him a Peter Pan and he'd laughed at what was, of course, intended as a joke.

He fought incessantly against these depressing thoughts and ideas. He knew them to be untrue. He had wanted to help children, more and more children (why even Willy had said exactly the same thing about him only the other day to someone) because, for God's sake, he wanted to serve humanity.

'I couldn't bear to live and not even try to do some good in the world; to die without having done something worthwhile.'

This was his 'rule' and he had stuck to it. Then why did the past torment him so? The failure of the 'hundred houses' scheme, the failure of attempts to make money from property development, money destined for helping children.

He re-lived all his old failures, many of them now quite imaginary for he was in a state (and he knew it) of mournful depression and loss. He re-lived even that far-off, dreadful time when he had to walk through a village street and people shouted after him and called him names.

They had not been able to harm him then, but in retrospect, the harm with its poison began to work inside him.

Perhaps the one idea which tormented him most was that perhaps he had failed in rearing the children. In sleepless nights he asked himself again and again the question: had it all been worthwhile? Perhaps the children would have survived anyway without him? Perhaps they would have avoided the troubles they'd encountered? So many troubles! Terry, Willy, Paul, Babs . . . was he in some obscure way to blame? Had he been too indulgent or too strict? How would 'natural' parents have behaved?

He had given his youth, his 'best' ten years; how terrible if it were all mistaken!

Denise was worried about Uncle's appetite. He was eating so little; it hardly seemed enough to sustain that enormous frame of his.

The girls, Pam, Margaret, Linda, Denise and Babs discussed the situation among themselves. Pam said: 'Uncle is always in a bad mood.' But all recognized the symptoms were more serious than a mood.

Margaret kept up her telephone calls, from the office where she worked.

His diary noted it: January 5th—'Margaret was never more encouraging than today. She went on and on about the possibilities ahead. But somewhere down the line is this extraordinary notion that I won't get anywhere *ever*. How much to move me? How much to persuade me? She keeps saying that I must lay the ghosts of the past and prove they're false. Going up in the car today, she really gave so much eagerness herself. It makes me very angry to watch myself fooling about.'

January 6th—'Hopeless me! I need a Margaret to keep me going eagerly or I lose the bounce.'

January 10th—'Went to London to look for flats or offices. Went to see one in W1.'

January 14th—'Last year certainly was an upheaval year —up, down, crash, success, all in one. Perhaps a year of great opportunity to learn. Seven years technical and legal clearing up. Linda married. Margaret began to establish herself in own career. Paul survived another difficult year. Finance straightened out, decks cleared, so to speak, and the new hope of one's worst failures pointing to a new hope of doing better. What can one contribute? How to take one's talents and use them?'

February 5th—'Decided to take a flat in London. Spent the month buying necessary and additional furniture for it. Wrote some articles. Wrote a piece on bringing up children for Woman's Hour which they are going to do on the radio.'

February 27th—'I have to admit a heavy depression. Am in totally confused position of having no flat of my own at Lovelocks and a flat in London, but no knowledge of how things will go for me.'

July—'Returned to Lovelocks to practise singing . . . went to Lourdes.' August—'Went out with a friend in London.' And then, in September—'Feeling very depressed, my scalp trouble getting worse again; my appetite appallingly

bad; almost all my early New Year interests washed away;
my spirits fell very low. Giving up the London flat; pointless
to keep it any longer.'

October 24th—'Removal day at the flat. Babs came to
town with me and we emptied the flat and cleaned it up.'

35

Uncle is Himself Again

It was spring again. Margaret was in love and came down at weekends to talk about it. To plan for a summer wedding, with Father Woolmer, of course, presiding.

Suddenly Peter found himself busier than ever before. There was Margaret's twenty-first birthday party to prepare. Even Dink had little time to spare to help him. All the girls were married or seriously in love now with someone. Each day brought the threat of a new engagement—either with a party to celebrate, or a tearful parting. Partings, where Pam, Christine, Brian and Paul were concerned, could last twenty-four hours, or forever. If it was forever, there was a new face and new hair-do to be encountered in front of the TV set or in the kitchen drinking coffee.

'Uncle, this is Bill,' one of the girls would say.

He tried to remember the names because if Peter said 'Good evening Charles' to someone and it wasn't, Christine got upset. Pam quite enjoyed it. 'Uncle, it's BILL, not . . . er . . . Eric.'

The house was full of laughter, as in the old days.

'Uncle,' said Denise, 'you ate all that steak-and-kidney pie I made you! I told you not to worry, didn't I. Parents always DO worry and fret. Honest, I don't know why.'

Peter just smiled. Suddenly, he felt relaxed and happy. Could it be the new car he'd set his heart on? He was, he knew it, quite mad on fast cars.

Really, he didn't seem to have a free moment nowadays. He felt a rush of warm gratitude to the girls for having encouraged him. He'd ordered a new canvas and started work on a new painting.

'You know,' he said to Denise one day, 'it must be this house of love. What with each one of you girls in love . . . It does make a difference.'

Babs was in the kitchen that day. To borrow the vacuum-cleaner, some sugar and a few tins of something.

'D'you remember Uncle, that time in Wales, giving me and Pam that great long sex talk; and we neither of us had a bloody clue.'

'You were both rather dense,' Peter said.

Babs said, 'You or Denise won't mind looking after baby for me this evening will you? I won't be late. Promise.'

'Sorry' said Peter, and Babs' face fell. 'As a matter of fact, I'm going to be awfully busy today. I'm writing a musical.'

'A what?'

'Uncle's bought an electric organ,' said Denise, 'he went went up to Harrods for it.'

'So if you stay in,' Peter said, 'you can both come and listen in my room tonight. I've written twenty-two pieces of music, with lyrics for fifteen of them. I've already sung and recorded the lyrics on to tape.'

Peter swept out of the kitchen. In a few moments, the girls could hear faint sounds of music coming from Uncle's room.

'You could bloody knock me down with a feather,' said Babs in her virile way. 'What's come over Uncle?'

'I'll look after Karen tonight' said Denise, 'but I'm glad you've noticed. Uncle is a different man lately.'

Linda came into the kitchen with her new baby daughter. 'Where's Uncle?'

'Listen,' Denise said.

Babs giggled.

'Never you mind,' Linda said, 'you wait till it's played by violins and drums and things. Won't it be marvellous if Uncle is better at it than . . . anyone!'

'Uncle's as good, nearly, as the Beatles,' said Dink loyally.

The morning of Margaret's 21st party was bright. The old house was filled with sunlight. Peter started by putting jars of daisies and bluebells in every room. In the sitting-room, he arranged the pick of the flowers with great yellow pansies and irises, framed in laurel leaves. He stood back to get the full effect. Nice.

Margaret drifted downstairs in her filmy pale lemon negligee, looking still half asleep with her pale face and dark eyes. Peter knew he'd have the next hour or so with all the latest news and views about 'lovely Len'. However once Margaret really got started with the cream and jam sponge and all the scones she was going to make, the work would be done in lightning fashion. It would take him far longer to clean up the kitchen afterwards. Besides he liked Margaret's 'suitor' Len Corbin, an American teacher, an attractive, intellectual blond young man.

'Blast' said Peter, 'the lettuce and cress will run out long before I finish these open sandwiches.' He was cutting thin slices and decorating them with a variety of cream-cheeses, slivers of olive and gherkin, hard-boiled egg and tomato with a sprinkling of cress and shredded lettuce.

Brian who was having a late breakfast because it was Saturday, said: 'Uncle how much did you pay in the village for that greenstuff?'

Peter said lettuce was still expensive at one-and-sixpence each and tenpence for the cress.

'I'll get my bike' Brian said, 'I'll be back in a jiffy with some more stuff. Say half-a-crown then.'

'I'll pay you later,' Peter said.

Margaret was patting her hair in front of a mirror. 'I'll just get dressed, Darling Uncle dearest, then I'll start work. It won't take me long. Lenny, thank God, is nothing like Brian. He's not . . . commercial at all,' Margaret shuddered.

Ten minutes later Brian was back in the kitchen, holding out a small rather limp lettuce and a lot of cress crushed in a newspaper.

'My' said Peter, 'you were quick. You must have flown to the village and back.'

'Don't mention it' Brian said, 'I like to help Uncle, any way I can.'

'Why . . . you so-and-so Brian,' Margaret said as she floated out of the kitchen and upstairs, 'you've been at Simon's vegetable patch again.'

'No quarrelling today,' Peter declaimed in a lordly sort of voice. 'Remember all of you, it's Maggie's birthday . . .'

Paul arrived to make himself coffee and toast. 'Can I help, Uncle please?'

He agreed to peel ten pounds of large old potatoes.

'Thanks old man' said Peter. He and Paul were now close friends.

Several hours later, Peter said everyone was to stop and have some refreshment. The kitchen was warm and glowing with sun and Margaret's sponge cakes. There were telephone calls from Willy and Terry who said they hoped to be in time for the party. A hand-painted card arrived from John.

Peter felt an unexpected rush of emotion. He went out into the back garden and called to the upstairs window.

'Linda . . . all of you, come to the kitchen, I'm going to hand round a celebration drink.'

He spread glasses, some kitchen ones and some 'best' on the kitchen table and poured some wine into each. Pam and Christine, long hair undone or swathed in towels from the bathroom where they'd been washing it, to be special for the party.

Peter raised his glass and his eyes met Paul's.

'Speech, Uncle' said Paul.

'Yes speech' they all said.

A loud wail from Linda's baby broke the tension. Peter embraced Margaret. After all, it was an emotional day for him; his eldest girl's twenty-first.

'All right kids; no speech,' he raised his glass to each in turn. 'Just thank you. Thank all of you. For being you.'

Pam said: 'Uncle, you look different . . . as though something nice had happened to you.'

'Ah' said Peter who felt he'd had enough emotion for one day, however happy a feeling it was. And the party not yet even begun! 'Ah, that's because I've got myself a present and it's not even my birthday. Actually, it's in the garage now . . .'

Brian, the fastest runner—if only he'd worked at it, Peter thought, watching him streak off—was there first, shrieking his head off.

Peter followed with the rest of the family. He was holding Angela in his arms, while Linda held her baby.

'Uncle' Brian shouted, 'yippee, a bloody Bentley Convertible. Uncle, how MUCH? And how . . . ?'

'How?' shrieked all the children, 'did you get it?'

'Well, only second-hand,' said Peter modestly.

Suddenly, he knew everything was going to be all right. These children were his; better than that though, they were —all of them—on HIS side.

EPILOGUE

The last word goes to Denis Allen.

'In my opinion it's a success,' Denis Allen told me. 'I told you; we took a chance on our hunch and it's worked. I might not take such a chance again.

'You've got to remember the important thing is that Peter Jeffcock gave these children the love and individual care they needed. That means that it's fairly certain they in their turn will be able to give love and care to THEIR children.

'You can ignore the fact that sometimes the youngsters got into trouble. You'll see, they'll get over it and grow up to have a successful life and to marry and love their children. What else matters?

'The point is, they needed someone and Peter was there to supply that need. Above all, Peter Jeffcock needed to BE needed.'

I think Denis Allen is right.